Tuna on the Fly

Tuna on the Fly

A Comprehensive Guide
to Fly Fishing's
Ultimate Trophy Fish

Tom Gilmore

The Countryman Press
Woodstock, Vermont

Library of Congress Cataloging-in-Publication Data
Data has been applied for.

ISBN 10: 0-88150-635-4
ISBN 13: 978-0-88150-635-8

Jacket photo © Dave Skok
Jacket design by Johnson Design, Inc.
Text design by Faith Hague Book Design
Text composition by Susan Livingston
Maps by Paul Woodward, © The Countryman Press
Illustrations by Barbara Smullen and Brian R. Schneider
Photo on page 17 by Tom Richardson, page 85 by Gene Quigley,
    page 135 by Jeff Pierce, and page 187 by Tom Gilmore

Published by The Countryman Press,
P.O. Box 748, Woodstock, VT 05091

Distributed by W. W. Norton & Company, Inc.,
500 Fifth Avenue, New York, NY 10110

Printed in the United States of America

10 9 8 7 6 5 4 3 2 1

To Mom
Although our time together was much too short,
it was long enough for you to instill your values in me
and for me to learn what is really important in life.

Contents

Acknowledgments

Over the years, so many people have contributed to my knowledge and enjoyment of the sport of fly fishing and to the publication of this manuscript. I wish I could individually acknowledge each and every one of them, but time and space do not allow. So let me first thank all the anglers, tiers, and friends not mentioned below.

In the pages that follow, I tell a few stories about catching my first of several species of tuna, and you never forget your first. I wish to extend my deepest appreciation to the captains who guided me to my firsts:

Steve Bellefleur, who skillfully guided me nearly two decades ago to my first two species of fly-rod tuna—bonito and false albacore. Steve generously shares his knowledge and his keen sense of humor with all his charters. Steve, you're simply the best; see you on the water.

Scott Hamilton, who put me onto my first blackfin tuna and introduced me to the phenomenal summer run of false albacore off Palm Beach, Florida. Scott, no one works as hard as you do. I look forward to seeing you at our annual albie fest.

Jaime Boyle, who set out on a mission and guided me to my first fly-rod bluefin hours after our charter was due to end. Jaime, thank you for making me stick with it.

Scott Avanzino, who expertly maneuvered his boat, *Balancing Act*—and it was a balancing act—around a giant oil rig and away from a massive bull shark as I was fighting my first yellowfin. The 65-pound fish eventually ended up in his cooler. Scott not only knows how to catch tuna but also how to have fun and a great day on the water.

Terry Nugent, who guided me toward the thrill of victory and who graciously shared with me the ultimate agony of defeat as I lost my biggest tuna to date—boatside. Terry, you'll always be a hero in my book.

To Ed Jaworowski, friend and mentor. Ed, thanks for constantly setting the bar high and always taking my fishing to the next level. Thanks also for the great photographs of the flies that grace the pages of this book. To Peter McCarthy, for organizing bluefin trips to Cape Cod and for reviewing this entire manuscript. Peter, thank you for your thoughtful suggestions and for your support and encouragement along the way. To Ed Janiga, for initially pushing me to put down the rod and pick up the pen. To Joe Darcy, my silent partner, who quietly adds so much to every trip and makes the enjoyment of this sport just that much better. To Howard Woodbury, Lenny Maiorano, and Teddy Patlen, for, well, just being Woody, Lenny, and Teddy—great friends and great fun.

Special thanks to Captain Gene Quigley, who helped in every aspect of this book, lending his knowledge, flies, photos, and editorial comments on the Mid-Atlantic chapter. Bill Dawson, for his support and help in obtaining the great tackle used to do the "field research" for this project: Sage rods, Tibor and Ross reels, and Rio lines, all top-of-the-line tuna tackle. Greg Skomal, Dr. Barbara Block, and Dr. Molly Lutcavage, scientists who have dedicated their careers to providing the science so that we have the opportunity to conserve our natural treasures. Thank you for so generously sharing your knowledge and for your lifelong commitment to conserving tuna.

Jeff Pierce, sales manager for Mustad & Son, for sharing his knowledge, insight, photos, and flies. Brian Schneider, for his youthful enthusiasm and for his illustrations used in this publication. For help and support with the photos, Michael Schweit, Gary Graham (owner of Baja on the Fly), Scott Barnes, Art Morris, Pete Bacinski, Dave Skok, and Captains Joe LeClair, Steve Moore, Tommy Rapone, Sandy Noyes, Tom Richardson, Sarah Gardner, and Brian Horsley.

For supplying the flies used in the book, Dave Skok, Rich Murphy, Blane Chocklett, and Captains Nat Moody and Derek Spengler.

To fellow anglers Jack Radigan, Bill Ryan, Joe Johnston, Larry Bucciarelli, Steve Murphy, Joe Keegan, Joey DiBello, Rickey Stevens, Matt Toomey, Lee Schisler, Matt Spengler, Pete Douma, Mitch Nottingham, Jim Levison, and Joe Pheifer. Thanks, guys, for the great times and the memories.

To the four-dozen guides who shared their knowledge, experience, and hot spots with me. They formed the foundation for this book, and I want to acknowledge their contributions.

For their help on the Northeast chapter, Captains Joe LeClair, Terry Nugent, Steve Moore, Jaime Boyle, Tommy Rapone, Ken and Lori Vanderlaske, Nat Moody, Derek Spengler, Dave Preble, Al Anderson, Corey Pietraszek, John Pirie, Bob Paccia, Steve Bellefleur, Steve Burnett, and Sandy Noyes.

For information about the Mid-Atlantic region, Captains Gene Quigley, Bill Hoblitzell, Al Ristori, Anthony Grassi, Frank Crescitelli, Joe Mustari, Chris Hessert, Jim Levison, and John McMurray.

The Southeast chapter would not have been possible without the help of Captains Steve Coulter, Dickie Harris, Scott Hamilton, Jeff Burns, Russ Multz, Ken Harris, Keith Winter, and Joey Dawson.

For the chapter on the Gulf of Mexico, Captains Mike Thierry, Tommy Pellegrin, Scott Avanzino, Lance Walker, Peace Marvel, and Charlie Stetzel.

Special thanks to the crew at Ramsey Outdoors—Stuart Levine, Bill Tomiello, and John Roetman—for their ongoing support of fishing clubs and their commitment to promoting the sport of fly fishing through their annual series of educational seminars. These seminars are free to all and are dedicated to increasing our knowledge and enjoyment of the sport.

For his crisp editing of my early drafts, I'd like to thank my colleague Walter Keonig. I am grateful to Jennifer Thompson, Darren Brown, and Kermit Hummel of the Countryman Press for their continued support of my work.

To my three beautiful daughters and their husbands—Jennifer and Jim, Julie and Darren, Chrissy and Bryan—great kids and great friends. To my adorable grandchildren, and hopefully future anglers—Jack (six), Ashley (five), Reagan (three), and Paige (nine months)—for making every family get-together a joy and for the beautiful artwork that decorated my draft manuscripts. To my daughters' in-laws—Don and Eileen, Joe and Jo Ann, and Joni—for always asking about my fishing trips but never acknowledging that they think my fishing obsession is just a bit insane.

Most of all I want to thank my wife, Joanne. As my lifelong partner, she has always supported my passion for fishing and the outdoors. She is my partner in everything I do, especially in my writing; she reviews, questions, edits, and improves every sentence I write. This book would not have been possible without her loving help, wisdom, and support.

The author with a bluefin tuna off the Rhode Island coast

TOM GILMORE

Introduction

I have been fortunate enough to travel extensively to fly fish for most of the world's highly prized sport fish. I know the exhilarating feeling you get when you hear the violent ripping sound your backing makes as it cuts through the water following a bonefish across a glass-smooth tropical flat and off into the horizon. Monster tarpon have taken my breath away with their gill-rattling aerial displays. My heart has been broken by the brute strength of a king salmon's powerful run down a raging Alaskan river as I helplessly watched the last few turns of my backing melt off the reel.

All these were incredibly memorable fishing experiences, but none were even in the same league as the thrill, excitement, and challenge of tackling tuna on the fly. I still remember feeling the agony of defeat after losing my first fly-rod bluefin tuna boatside following a brutal battle that lasted well over an hour. That loss left me with an empty feeling that nagged me for almost a year, until I was able to return to the scene of the crime to triumphantly land my first fly-rod bluefin. Memories of that success now bring a warm, satisfying glow.

In the tranquil and serene world of fly fishing, we usually don't conjure up violent images like blitzing rockets, torpedoes, freight trains, mortar shots, and bullets, but fly fishing for tuna is extreme fly fishing. It's a fly fisher's version of running a marathon, climbing Mount Everest, or biking in the Tour de France. A few years back, just the thought of tackling tuna on a fly would have qualified you as temporarily insane.

In the fall of 1991, Steve Able chartered a 113-foot boat, the *Royal Polaris,* out of San Diego, California, for the first well-publicized big-game bluewater fly-fishing trip. Numerous world records were broken on that momentous trip, especially for yellowfin and skipjack tuna. Steve Able, in addition to creating the Able series of fly reels, which is still one of the industry standards for excellence, was one of the early pioneers of bluewater fly fishing, and his 1991 trip launched a new era in the sport of saltwater fly fishing.

For the purposes of this book, which covers fly fishing for tuna from the Gulf of Maine to the Gulf of Mexico, I define bluewater as the warm offshore waters in and around the Gulf Stream.

For the Record

In the last decade, the popularity of fly fishing for tuna has spread along the entire East Coast of North America and throughout the Gulf of Mexico. Seventy percent of the International Game Fish Association (IGFA) fly-rod tippet-class world records for tuna have been broken in that time. The percentage is even higher for two of our larger tuna, yellowfin (82 percent, 9 of 11 tippet-class records) and bluefin (87 percent, 7 of 8 tippet-class records). Several of these records have been broken repeatedly; for example, the bluefin 20-pound tippet class has fallen three times since 1996.

It should be noted that big-game bluewater fly fishing is not a male-dominated sport. All five of the yellowfin female tippet-class records have been broken since 1998, with several new 16- and 20-pound tippet, class records. In 2005 alone there were three new female tippet-class records for bluefin.

Tackle manufacturers are responding to an increased demand for sturdier gear, and fly-fishing stores are reporting greater numbers of 12- and 14-weight outfits passing through their doors. Many manufacturers are designing reels with larger line capacities and tougher drag systems, and fly lines are being constructed with stronger cores in order to tackle tuna and other offshore big-game species.

PETER MCCARTHY

Outlasting a large tuna is not for the faint of heart.

Saltwater fly fishing is the fastest growing sector of the industry. Chasing the smaller inshore tuna, bonito, and false albacore has become so popular that in some areas these fish have cultlike followings. Groups of anglers make annual albie pilgrimages to such famous destinations as Martha's Vineyard, Massachusetts; Montauk, New York; Harkers Island, North Carolina; and, more recently, Palm Beach, Florida.

While researching my book *False Albacore: A Comprehensive Guide to Fly Fishing's Hottest Fish,* published by the Countryman Press in the fall of 2002, I had the pleasure of fishing with many guides who also target false albacore's larger cousins—blackfin, bluefin, and yellowfin tuna. On more than one occasion, I had the thrill of hooking and landing several of these great fish. So it seemed like a natural progression for me to kick it up a notch and tackle *Tuna on the Fly.*

Bluewater fly fishing is still in its infancy. There is so much yet to be discovered about fly fishing's newest frontier. In the pages that follow, I share what I have learned about fly fishing for tuna, along with tips from some of the finest tuna guides and most dedicated fly fishermen in North America.

My hope is that you will join the growing number of anglers who treasure these magnificent creatures and that you will join me in advocating global cooperation for sustaining viable populations of tuna for future generations to enjoy, both as sport fish and table fare.

Part I

Fly Fishing for Tuna

The Fish

I started saltwater fly fishing in the Northeast during the late 1970s, when the striped bass population was starting to crash. So bluefish were my primary target back then. Bluefish are considered the junkyard dog of saltwater fish—they are mean, tough, and aggressive predators. When you hook one, hold on tight, because they just bear down and slug it out from the instant they strike until you release them. I have enormous respect for the determination of bluefish.

By the early 1980s, the populations of striped bass were so depleted that in 1984 Congress passed the Striped Bass Recovery Act. This eliminated most commercial harvests and greatly restricted recreational limits. Subsequently, striped bass started coming back, and in such good numbers that I fell in love with them all over again.

They offered me everything I could want in a fish. They were large, strong, and beautiful and would take a fly. They weren't easy to catch, often being superselective, providing this veteran "match the hatch" trout fisherman with plenty of challenges. For years, I felt that no other fish could ever replace my beloved striped bass. During the early 1990s, they seemed so abundant that I felt I was experiencing the good old days, and nothing could take me away from bass. I wanted to get my fill of fishing for this great creature before man, progress, politics, and greed drove their numbers back down again.

Bombs Away

Then the unexpected happened. On one of my fall striper outings, I saw a school of fish literally exploding out of the water chasing frantic little baitfish. I had never seen fish attack prey species so viciously. It looked like someone was firing cannonballs into the helpless schools of bay anchovies. Then in an instant the fray was over. The fish quickly vanished, only to show a few seconds later far into the distance, again throwing whitewater and baitfish high into the air.

I found out later that the explosions were blitzing tuna, in this case little tunny (*Euthynnus alletteratus*). Since no self-respecting fly fisher would want to fish for a "little" anything, most anglers refer to *E. alletteratus* as false albacore, which is the common name I use throughout this book. We never got the opportunity to cast to those ocean predators that day, but their speed and violent explosions on their prey captivated me. I became determined to target tuna on the fly.

Although saltwater fly fishing was growing in popularity in the early 1990s, there were very few full-time saltwater fly-fishing guides in the Northeast and Mid-Atlantic states, and those that did exist were hard to locate. These were the days before the Internet and saltwater fly-fishing magazines.

It wasn't until I met Captain Steve Bellefleur, who guides out of Stonington, Connecticut, that I was able to begin targeting the small inshore tuna. Steve generously shared his passion for and knowledge of inshore tuna and guided me to my first Atlantic bonito and false albacore. The more I fished for these inshore tuna, the more I became intrigued by them.

The inshore fishing season in the Northeast is short and often interrupted by storms that further limit the number of days for tuna fishing. Craving more tuna time, I started booking guides at other East Coast tuna hot spots from the northern Gulf of Maine to the Gulf of Mexico. On these excursions I met other tuna fanatics and guides who were pushing the envelope by targeting the larger tuna species—blackfin, yellowfin, and the king of all tuna, the bluefin.

By fishing farther offshore, I found I could extend my tuna season in the Northeast by an extra few weeks, and by following the Gulf Stream south to North Carolina's Outer Banks, the Florida Keys, and the Gulf of Mexico, it was possible to fish for tuna year-round without leaving the United States. That is not to say that I fish all 12 months; family and professional commitments preclude such a fantasy. But it's comforting to know that anytime I can stow away a few days to fish, tuna will be waiting for me somewhere along the East Coast or Gulf Coast.

In Part III, Hot Spots and Happy Hours, I discuss in detail where to find tuna year-round, but first let's take a closer look at what makes a tuna tick.

Built for Speed

Tuna is the common name for several large, oceanic species of *Thunnus* and related genera, of the family Scombridae, order Perciformes. They are great roamers, capable of incredibly long migrations. Tuna have been clocked swimming at speeds of over 50 mph. In fact, the English word "tuna" is derived from the Greek verb *thuno*, which means "to rush," referring to their hurried lifestyle. Members of the tuna family are nearly all muscle, with upwards of 75 percent of their body weight being muscle mass, compared to less than 40 percent for most fish.

Tuna have a higher proportion of red muscle than any other fish. Red muscles are built for fast, long endurance runs. That is why angling battles with large tuna are often referred to as marathons; they are exhausting but exhilarating, potentially lasting for hours. Tuna are hydrodynamic marvels, with a sleek, rounded, streamlined, torpedo-shaped body that is built for sustained speed. Their dorsal and pectoral fins are recessed and can retract into groves to reduce friction. Their pectoral fins, when not recessed, act like wings and are used for gliding, turning, and

JOE LECLAIR

Aided by their torpedo-shaped bodies, tuna are the fastest fish on the planet.

providing lift. Tuna have small, smooth scales and eyes that form a smooth surface with the rest of the head, all evolved to reduce drag.

Most fish are cold-blooded; their internal body temperature matches that of the surrounding water. Tuna, on the other hand, are warm-blooded. Their well-developed vascular system keeps their body temperature higher than the water they inhabit. A higher body temperature allows for faster metabolism, which enables the red muscles of the tuna to contract much more quickly, permitting them to swim faster after prey. Giant bluefin tuna are the "hottest" of all tuna, capable of maintaining their body temperature as high as 35 degrees Fahrenheit above the water temperature. This lets them expand their range farther into cooler northern waters in search of food.

Unlike fish that swim by moving their body back and forth in a sort of wigglelike motion, tuna propel themselves forward by moving only their powerful, widely forked, rudderlike tail, which can cycle up to 30 times per second. The rest of the body stays straight like a torpedo. Scientists refer to this as thunniform swimming. For short distances, billfish are slightly faster than tuna, but when it comes to sustained speed, tuna are the fastest fish on the planet.

These fish have no respiratory mechanism to ensure flow of oxygen-bearing water over the gills; only the movement caused by swimming achieves this. They must swim continuously with an open mouth to pass oxygen over their gills to breathe. The slowest a tuna can safely swim to maintain oxygen flow is equivalent to the length of its own body every second—faster than the fastest human swimmer at top speed.

Tuna don't have gas or swim bladders, which make fish buoyant. They are negatively buoyant, meaning they must literally sink or swim, and they would die if they stopped swimming. Engineers from several leading universities have studied the tuna's hydrodynamic body to try to improve the design of submarines. At the Massachusetts Institute of Technology, scientists have tried to build a replica "robotuna" in the hopes of inventing a more efficient underwater vehicle.

The tunas have a relatively small stomach, yielding more body weight to muscle. Because of this and their fast metabolism, they must consume a high percentage of their body weight daily in prey species. This makes them almost continual eating machines, which is a real plus for anglers. Research on stomach contents show that they feed throughout the water column, on both pelagic (open ocean) and bottom fishes. Favorite foods include hake, peanut bunker, sand eels, silversides, bay anchovy, herring, mackerel, flying fish, and squid.

Eye of an Eagle

While tuna are ferocious eaters, don't assume they are easy to fool with a fly. Tuna have keen eyesight and can be leader-shy and extremely selective when feeding. The eyes of most fish are placed so widely apart that each eye collects separate uncoordinated images, and the brain processes them as two separate images. This is called monocular vision. Tuna, like many highly developed predators such as hawks, owls, tigers, and wolves—and humans as well—have eyes in the front of their heads, giving them a wide field of overlapping vision. The brain processes these images as one, resulting in what is called binocular vision. Binocular vision allows a more accurate assessment of the exact location of prey species.

Blackfin (*Thunnus atlanticus*)

Tackle Junkie

I must confess to being quite the tackle junkie. The last two fly rods I purchased were a 3-weight and a 16-weight, as I already owned everything in between. Justifying the need to own over two-dozen fly rods to my wife wasn't easy. First I tried telling her that I fish virtually every type of water there is, from little mountain brooks to the hallowed waters of the Catskills in New York, big western rivers, tropical flats, rock jetties, and breachways of the Northeast and bluewater from the Gulf of Maine to the Gulf of Mexico.

When that didn't seem to work, I escorted her to our oldest daughter's bedroom, opened the closet door, pointed to a huge line of shoes, and said, "Fly rods are to men what shoes are to most women." I think this analogy helped promote greater understanding of the battle of the sexes in the Gilmore household.

My good friend and colleague Lee Schisler, by comparison, is old school, a by-product no doubt of growing up in the remote mountains of north-central Pennsylvania. Despite being a veteran saltwater fly fisherman, Lee owns only one saltwater fly rod and reel, which he uses to out-fish the rest of our gang on a regular basis. What Lee lacks in tackle, he more than makes up for with his understanding and knowledge of the natural world. He is an excellent hunter, fisherman, birder, and field naturalist.

If you dropped him in the middle of the Alaskan wilderness with just the clothes on his back and a Swiss Army knife, Lee would have no problem living off the land. A month later, he would arrive back in civilization with a tanned face, a well-groomed beard, and a few extra pounds on his midsection.

A few years back, I invited him to join Lenny Maiorano and me on our annual trip to Palm Beach, Florida, to tackle false albacore and blackfin tuna. Lee was aware of how great the albie fishing is off Palm Beach, so he jumped at the invitation. Until I told him that he could join us only on one condition: He had to upgrade his tackle for the trip. "No way! My tackle is just fine, thank you," he responded.

Lee's outfit consisted of a 9-foot, 10-weight fiberglass rod made by Garcia and a Pfleuger Medalist reel, an outfit I had sold him some 15 years ago. It had served me well for almost a decade, but I'd wanted to upgrade to a graphite rod and a reel with a tougher drag system. Lee had taken countless striped bass and bluefish and even a few large king salmon on this outfit. But this would be his first trip for tuna, and I simply couldn't convince him just how tough these fish would be. Striped bass, blues, and king salmon are great game fish, but a tuna will flat out smoke you.

Despite my constant ribbing during the weeks leading up to the trip, Lee remained confident that his tackle would be up to the task. Whenever I raised the issue of gear, I always received the same reply: "That rod has taken 30-pound stripers and a 40-pound king salmon. Those albies and blackfin tuna are half that size; what the hell can they do?" And my answer was also always the same: "You'll see, buddy; you'll see."

The three of us flew down to Palm Beach on a Sunday morning in late June. We planned to fish with Captain Scott Hamilton from Monday to Thursday. When we checked in to our rooms at the Sailfish Marina, the desk clerk handed me a note from Scott: "Hey, guys, I had a cancellation today; lots of blackfin around; give me a call if you want to give it a shot this afternoon." Before sharing the good news, I asked the clerk if I could use the phone. Lee looked concerned and asked if there was something wrong. "Wrong?" I said. "Hell, no, boys; we're going fishing!"

I left a message on Scott's answering machine, and within the hour he was tying his 21-foot Wahoo up to our dock. It had been a year since our last trip, but Scott started right off busting our chops as if we hadn't missed a day. He knew I had been ribbing Lee about his tackle, and he was good enough to bring an extra outfit as a backup. As we boarded the boat, he looked at Lee's rod and reel and said, "What the hell is that? Are you fishing for ladyfish [a Florida light-tackle favorite]?" Lee correctly figured that he was in for a long afternoon.

GENE QUIGLEY

It pays to have a few backup rods and reels.

Scott ran his boat out through the Lake Worth inlet and headed east toward the Gulf Stream, which is only a few miles offshore at Palm Beach. In fact, it's closer to shore here than anywhere else along the East Coast, giving small-boat owners an easy shot at some great bluewater fishing. After a short ride, Scott cut the motor and began chumming with dead pilchards. It didn't take long for the albies to start busting through the bait. When he switched over to chumming with live pilchards, the albies really went nuts, churning the water into a white froth.

We were about to cast to the albies when Scott hollered, "Blackfin!" Sure enough, there was a small pod of blackfin porpoising just beyond the albies. Instantly Lee and I fired casts toward the blackfin, and wouldn't you know it, his fly hit the water a split second before mine. On his first strip, he was tight to a respectable blackfin tuna.

From the moment of hookup, Lee acted like a tuna veteran, screaming, "Fish on! Fish on!" while grinning from ear to ear. However, his exuberance was short-lived. Seconds after hookup his drag blew out, causing the spool to overspin and his line to bind up. The sudden stop of line put way more pressure on the rod than it could take. It exploded at the ferrule just before the fly line's backing broke. In less than 15 seconds,

Lee had hooked a blackfin tuna, burned out a reel, broken a rod, and lost a fly line. After a moment of silence Scott asked, "So, Lee, tell me; how do you like fishing for tuna?" "Guess those little bastards are a mite tougher than I thought," Lee replied sheepishly.

Scott laughed as he pulled out the extra outfit he had brought for just such an emergency. He shook Lee's hand and said, "Welcome to the big leagues, son." For the next several hours, Scott had us into nonstop tuna action. We must have landed at least four-dozen fish. While most of them were albies in the 8- to 12-pound range, we did land a few blackfin between 15 and 20 pounds. Lee was more than impressed with the fighting ability of these small tuna, which he said fought harder pound for pound than any species of fish he'd ever caught.

Description

Blackfin tuna are incredibly beautiful fish. They have a deep purple back, with a prominent gold to yellow lateral band on their upper sides. Their lower sides are silvery and their belly milky white. Their pectoral fins are fairly long, reaching almost to the beginning of the second dorsal fin. And their finlets are dusky with only a trace of yellow, not bright lemon yellow like most other tunas'. While blackfin have a robust fusiform body, they are one of the smaller tuna, with a maximum weight of 45 pounds and an average of 10 to 20 pounds.

Distribution and Behavior

Blackfin tuna are one of the few tuna with a limited migratory range. They prefer waters of about 70 degrees Fahrenheit or warmer, with the optimum around 74 degrees. Seasonally they can be found in the western Atlantic Ocean as far north as southern New England, but usually they range from North Carolina to Brazil, including the Caribbean and the Gulf of Mexico.

They most often feed on the surface, sometimes mixing with skipjack, in extremely large schools, which can churn the water into a white froth. Seabirds spot these feeding frenzies at great distances and are quick to join in the feast. Blackfin can be found wherever baitfish are likely to gather—over wrecks, over man-made structures such as gas rigs, along lines of current, and over reefs and banks. The best bite usually occurs during low-light conditions, and fishing is often better on cloudy days.

Tuna and seabirds trail in the wake of a trawler.

Unlike bluefin and yellowfin tuna, which can often be found in specific places at certain times of the year, blackfin are tireless wanderers within tropical waters. A location can be great one day and barren the next day. Hunting for blackfin can be like finding the proverbial needle in a haystack, unless you are lucky enough to find shrimp boats. Shrimp boats troll all night and cull their bycatch at first light. Tuna and other predators often follow in their wake, anticipating this enormous chum line.

Life History

Data on the reproductive biology of blackfin is lacking, but it is believed that their spawning grounds are located well offshore. Off the coast of Florida, their spawning season extends from April to November, with a peak in May. In the Gulf of Mexico, spawning lasts from June to September. Both sexes are thought to be sexually mature at two years of age, at which time they weigh about 5 or 6 pounds. Their current population seems to be stable, most likely due to their ability to reproduce at such a young age.

Blackfin are great fun on a fly rod.

Fly Fishing

If you have had the thrill of landing false albacore or bonito on a fly and you want to kick it up a notch, or if you are just starting out with tuna on the fly, I suggest that you target blackfin before you tussle with their larger cousins, yellowfin or bluefin. Blackfin tuna most often feed at or near the surface, making them excellent fly-rod quarry. For fish up to 15 or 20 pounds, a 10-weight rod is sufficient. If you plan to target blackfin frequently, you should consider investing in a 12-weight rod, as fish over 20 pounds are fairly common. And you never know when a yellowfin might be in the mix. Although blackfin don't have large teeth, they can cut a tippet, so I highly recommend fluorocarbon shock tippet.

Hot Spots

By far, the best blackfin tuna fishing is in the Florida Keys and throughout the Gulf of Mexico. Blackfin are in this region year-round, but the fishing usually peaks in spring and summer. If the fish are not visible, most captains anchor up-current from seamounts, offshore wrecks, or anywhere that structure causes an upwelling of water and then chum to bring the fish within casting range. In the gulf, a popular method is to target shrimp boats as they cull their bycatch. Also, night fishing for blackfin can be very productive around lighted oil rigs, which are magnets for baitfish.

Records

If you look at the world records, you'll see that Florida is the place to go for big blackfin. The IGFA all-tackle record blackfin tuna of 45 pounds 8 ounces was landed by Sam Burnett off Key West on May 4, 1996. There are currently 18 IGFA line-class world records for blackfin: 14 from Florida, 3 from Bermuda, and 1 from Puerto Rico. The fly-rod record is 34 pounds 3 ounces and was taken off Islamorada on December 17, 1977, by Rip Cunningham. Eight of the 10 fly-rod records are also from Florida.

Current IGFA Fly-Rod Records for Blackfin Tuna

Tippet	Weight (lbs./oz.)	Location	Angler	Date
Male				
2	Vacant			
4	2/0	Islamorada, FL	Vic Gaspeny	6/30/88
6	21/14	Argus Bank, Bermuda	Colin Rose	7/14/99
8	29/0	Tarpon Springs, FL	Luis R. Oliver	5/14/95
12	30/4	Key West, FL	John D. Kreinces	5/26/96
16	34/3	Islamorada, FL	Rip Cunningham	12/17/77
20	30/0	Walker's Cay, Bahamas	David Webb	6/20/92
Female				
2	Vacant			
4	Vacant			
6	22/4	Key West, FL	LuAnne Liederman	5/10/99
8	Vacant			
12	23/8	Key West, FL	Jennifer L. Andreae	5/13/99
16	25/0	Key West, FL	Mrs. William DuVal	4/29/00
20	28/6	Key West, FL	Linda P. Gracie	4/29/00

Yellowfin (*Thunnus albacares*)

3

This chapter was written a few weeks before Hurricane Katrina tragically struck the Gulf Coast, causing death and destruction of catastrophic proportions. After speaking with several of the guides I fish with out of Venice, Louisiana, I decided not to attempt a post-hurricane update. I hope you enjoy the story and that it will inspire you to fish down here. The guides and marinas in the region really need your support and would welcome your business.

Cursed

Blackfin and bluefin tuna have been very good to me, offering numerous legitimate fly-rod shots on virtually every outing. But for years yellowfin were an elusive treasure that I just couldn't connect with. Most of the time it wasn't even the fish that knocked me out of the game. Often it was the weather.

Yellowfin are a deepwater, offshore species, and fishing for them requires a decent-sized boat, a long boat ride, and a break from the weather. I've had several trips to the Gulf of Mexico and the Outer Banks of North Carolina canceled by storm fronts before I even left home in New Jersey—and these were the better trips. The killer trips were the ones where we actually arrived, only to find out that fast-moving fronts had wrecked our plans. On the rare occasion when the weather did cooperate, tackle failure or angler error seemed to rule the day.

I love to fish Hatteras Island on the Outer Banks, particularly in the fall after the tourists leave and you can enjoy the local flavor of the area.

But I'll never forget the four days and nights I spent cooped up with four of my closest fishing partners in two tiny, dark, damp motel rooms, and, I might add, neither will they.

Our alarm clocks would go off at 4:00 A.M. After a quick shower, we'd hurriedly grab a cup of coffee and a few doughnuts and go down to the marina to see if our captain had found a window in the weather that would allow us to get out to the Gulf Stream. Then, dejected with the news that we had lost yet another opportunity to tangle with tuna, we'd return to our rooms and watch the weather channel from sunup to sundown, looking for a ray of hope.

We repeated this ritual for four consecutive days. Finally, on the fifth day, we got a break—or so we thought. We met Captain Steve "Creature" Coulter at the dock, and he invited us aboard his 58-foot custom Carolina boat, *Sea Creature*. Steve started off by saying, "Well, boys, I can get you out to the Gulf Stream, and I can get you into some fish. However, it won't be comfortable, but it's up to you. But before you answer," he continued, "let me give you a piece of advice. When a captain says it won't be comfortable and it's up to you, your answer should always be, 'No, thanks; we will try another day.'"

I thanked Steve for his advice but pointed out to him that our nerves were getting raw, and that if we had to spend another 24 hours cooped up in those rooms, some lifelong friendships might be in jeopardy.

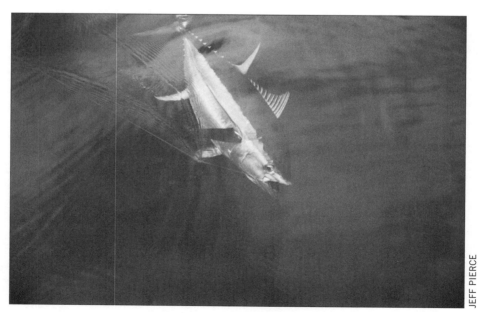

A yellowfin comes to the surface after a long battle.

As it turned out, Steve was right on all counts; we did get out to the Gulf Stream and we did catch some fish. But as much as I enjoy fishing for false albacore, they were not the hidden treasures we wanted to target with our 14-weight outfits. As for the discomfort, I can't bring myself to relive that day and those heaving seas, let alone share it with anyone else. Let me just say that for the first time in his life, the captain's mate kissed the dock when we landed.

This trip occurred about a month after my book *False Albacore* was published, and since I had interviewed Steve for the chapter on yellowfin and bluefin tuna, I thought I would give him a personalized copy. As I reached for my gear bag to get out the book, I asked Steve what he thought about albies. He looked at me with a scowl and growled, "I hate every one of those goddamned things!" Needless to say, I hastily shoved the book back into my bag. So is there anyone out there named Steve who'd like a free, personalized copy of *False Albacore?* There is one catch; your new nickname would have to be "Creature."

Finally!

After dozens of failed attempts at yellowfin on the fly, I decided to schedule a tuna trip to Venice, Louisiana, during early July, a period when the weather usually cooperates and cancellations are rare. While this is technically the beginning of hurricane season in the South, no hurricane had ever hit the United States during June or July for as long as the National Weather Service had been keeping records. I was counting on the weather gods, and the tuna gods, to finally smile down on me.

Getting a group together for my yellowfin excursions was becoming tougher and tougher, as word was spreading about my bad luck. Due to my risk-averse scheduling of a trip to the Gulf of Mexico in early July, I was able to convince fellow anglers Joe Darcy and Larry Bucciarelli to join me. They had previously come with me on only one yellowfin expedition, and that ranked as one of the better ones. (It was canceled by our guide, who called me on my cell phone as we neared our tenth hour in the car driving toward North Carolina's Outer Banks.)

We selected Joe Johnston to round out our foursome. Joe was an easy mark, since he was a new member of our fishing club, Coastal Flyrodders, and a tuna virgin who had no knowledge of my history with yellowfin.

With professional and family commitments, as well as my upcoming annual albie fest off Palm Beach, I had a very tight window to get down to Venice to fish for tuna and then fly on to West Palm Beach. After interviewing several top guides who fish out of Venice, I decided to schedule an overnight trip. It's a long run out to some of the deepwater rigs, so a 24-hour overnighter actually gives you more fishing time than two 12-hour trips because you have to make the long run to the fishing grounds only once.

The overnight trip also enables you to fish for tuna during the prime lowlight hours around sunset and sunrise. An additional bonus is fishing through the night, which can be magical for tuna. We booked a charter with Captain Scott Avanzino, who runs Paradise Outfitters, one of the more fly-rod friendly outfitters on the Gulf Coast.

Storm Warnings

Our plan was to fly down on Thursday afternoon, July 7, 2005, get a good night's sleep, and go out with Scott from midday Friday to midday Saturday. We would then fly to West Palm Beach on Sunday to join our fellow anglers in the hunt for false albacore. During the weeks leading up to our trip, I constantly monitored the weather and Venice's fishing reports. The reports confirmed that fishing was excellent, and the daily weather reports were carbon copies of each other—sunny, hot, and humid with a chance of afternoon showers, but light winds and calm seas.

That all changed early in the Fourth of July weekend. The National Weather Service was reporting that an angry young lady was about to visit New Orleans. Tropical Storm Cindy hit on Monday, July 4, with 70-mph winds and over 8 inches of rain. I called Scott on Tuesday morning to see if the aftereffects of Cindy would impact our fishing. Scott said that he thought the gulf seas would be settled by Friday, but that we might have an even bigger problem.

There were preliminary reports of a hurricane brewing in the Caribbean, and its core was projected to hit Louisiana Saturday afternoon. Scott said he was canceling all his charters between Cindy and impending Hurricane Dennis, but he felt there was a slim chance there would be a short fishable break between the two storms. Scott loves to fly fish, but he gets only a handful of fly charters a year. He promised that if a window did open up, he would offer it to us first.

The Window between Two Walls of Water

When I arrived at work on Wednesday morning, I had an urgent e-mail from Scott: "Tom, Cindy is through, and they are calling for light winds and 2- to 3-foot seas for Thursday and Friday. Hurricane Dennis isn't projected to hit Louisiana until Saturday afternoon. If you can move up your trip a day and get down here tomorrow afternoon, we might be able to pull off an overnight trip Thursday into Friday. Let me know your answer ASAP, so I can book the charter with a local group if you can't make it."

Our flight was scheduled for early Thursday morning, so getting there wasn't a problem. For me, "getting there" has never been the problem—getting out is another story. With my track record, asking my partners to fly from Newark, New Jersey, to New Orleans and then drive two hours to Venice hoping for a 24-hour window between two storms was not something I thought wise. Conventional wisdom would be to once again cancel my yellowfin trip. Like Yogi Berra, I was having the feeling of déjà vu all over again.

I shot Scott an e-mail telling him that I would check with my crew and get right back to him. I also inquired as to how the fishing was right before Cindy. His instant response was, "Great! If we get out, you'll get all the blackfin you want and hook some yellowfin, and if they are small enough, perhaps even land one on a fly." The thought of "all the blackfin you want" and the possibility of landing a yellowfin on a fly was enough for me to throw caution to the wind and relentlessly lobby my partners to take a chance.

Their responses were pretty much the same: "What the hell; it beats work, and getting stranded on Bourbon Street in New Orleans wouldn't be all that bad." Not wanting to risk that Scott would book another party, I left voice messages on his cell, home, and office phones in addition to e-mailing him. When I left work that Wednesday evening, I knew that in less than 24 hours we would be in Louisiana. What I didn't know was whether we would be sitting in the stern of Scott's 32-foot Albemarle Express Sportfisherman, *Balancing Act,* or stranded in a cheap hotel near the airport.

Not wanting to take any chances on our morning flight out of Newark, we arrived three hours before takeoff and checked our bags curbside. Prior to September 11, 2001, I had always carried my fishing gear on planes. Since 9/11, carrying reels with line has often been a problem for security, so I check them. Being the first on our flight to check bags, we assumed they would be the first off the plane. Our flight to New Orleans was on time and refreshingly uneventful. Shortly after arriving at the baggage claim, we saw several of our bags, and soon we had seven of our eight checked bags. The eighth, of course, was my gear bag containing eight reels, several hundred flies, leader material, rain gear, and two sets of Tarponwear.

The gentleman at baggage claim tried to be helpful and reassuring. He told us that my bag, which had been held back for a security check, would be on the next flight and arrive at my hotel by 8 P.M. However, if all went according to plan, we would be fishing in the middle of the Gulf of Mexico by then. This was quite a blow to us since, as the tackle junkie, I was supposed to provide flies and backup reels and lines for the trip. With the threat of a hurricane looming, to get out into the Gulf and back safely we really had no choice but to fish without my gear. Taking a quick inventory of what we did have in the way of tackle, we decided that we could get by.

The next step was to contact Scott to tell him we had landed and ask him for a weather update. He reported that Hurricane Dennis wasn't due to make landfall until Saturday afternoon, but cautioned that we should get to the marina as soon as possible because we would be fishing rigs that were 60 to 75 miles out in the gulf, in the direction of the approaching storm. Scott also suggested that we move our flight out of New Orleans from Sunday to Saturday morning to get out of Dodge before the hurricane hit. We changed our flights and went directly to the marina. There wasn't time to check in to our motel—we could do that after fishing.

The ride from the airport to Venice afforded us the opportunity to see firsthand the damage inflicted by Tropical Storm Cindy. Over twenty thousand homes were still without power, the streets were lined with debris, and many of the stores were still closed. The last weather report we heard before pulling into the marina was that Dennis, which was now blasting through Cuba with wind gusts up to 150 mph, had been upgraded to a Category 4 hurricane.

Dennis still wasn't scheduled to hit Louisiana until Saturday afternoon, but local officials were already asking residents to begin voluntary evacuations on Friday morning. According to the local press, the authorities didn't want a repeat of the massive traffic jams that occurred during the previous year's Hurricane Ivan.

No Gas, No Fish

After meeting Scott and his mate, Captain Lance Walker, we loaded our gear onto the *Balancing Act*. Scott told us that the marine forecast was still good—light winds and 1- to 2-foot seas. Although Dennis had us in its sights, it was traveling at only 15 mph and wasn't projected to get to Louisiana until almost 24 hours *after* we'd be off the water.

Scott seemed so confident that we'd hook up with blackfin and yellowfin that I finally began to believe my yellowfin tuna curse had been lifted. He suggested that we rig our rods while he motored over to the gas docks. He had about a half tank but needed to fill up before making the long run offshore.

We were next in line for gas when my curse appeared to have returned with a cruel twist: There was a loud pop, and the marina suddenly joined the twenty thousand other customers without electrical power. I assumed a marina that relies on electricity for its entire product line—gas, ice, bait, and cold drinks—would surely have a backup gas generator. Not so. Scott checked at the marina office, but they had no idea when power would be restored.

No power, no gas; no gas, no fish. I had gotten this far, only to find myself sitting on the dock without fuel at a Louisiana bayou on the Gulf of Mexico, which was teeming with tuna, and experiencing light winds and calm seas between two major weather systems.

It looked like it was happening again. I went up to the marina store, which was already beginning to warm up without air conditioning, and purchased a six-pack of barely chilled beer in a lame effort to cheer up the troops. If we didn't get power soon, we would be left with two choices: fish the bay for trout and redfish, or just turn around and head to Florida. I couldn't embrace either option.

I tried to remain positive in front of my friends, but I could tell from the looks in their eyes that they truly believed I was cursed—as did I. In a last desperate attempt at optimism, Larry offered to make a run to pick up a cooler for tuna steaks. About 20 minutes later, just as Larry came back down the road to the marina, the power came on. Scott quickly filled both tanks, and in a short time we were motoring out to the South Pass, past some 23 miles of marshland, and on to the gulf.

From there we headed southeast 53 miles to the Na Kika, a massive rig operated by British Petroleum. Prior to Tropical Storm Cindy, Scott had been having good success around this platform, which sits in about 5,000 feet of water. When we finally arrived at dusk, we could see tuna busting through bait all around the rig. The speed at which they were chasing bait to the surface was causing them to go airborne, and the sight of tuna up to 75 pounds flying through the air and crashing bait sent adrenalin rushing through our veins.

Scott suggested that I fish from the bow while two other anglers fished from the stern. When I got up to cast, aided by the lights from the

JEFF PIERCE

Offshore oil rigs are yellowfin magnets.

rig, I could see tuna slashing in every direction. I tossed my fly toward a boil, and on the second strip I was tight to a tuna. After a run of about 50 yards, my line went slack. I reeled in to find that the tippet had been frayed by one of the chicken dolphin we'd landed on the way out, causing me to lose the tuna.

Tuna fever was getting the better of us and we all committed a series of angling errors, including blown casts, missed strikes, and broken tippets. Gradually our nerves began to calm, and it wasn't long before blackfin tuna started coming over the gunwales two and three at a time.

Culling through Acres of Blackfin

Having caught blackfin in the Keys and off the east coast of Florida, and having enjoyed more than one grilled blackfin dinner, what happened next came as a complete shock. We didn't know it, but in the gulf blackfin aren't considered a quality game fish. As we brought one blackfin after another into the boat, our mate quickly sliced them up and tossed them into the chum bucket, telling us that they make excellent chum for yellowfin. After the mate had more than enough chum, we convinced him to release the rest of the blackfin we caught.

As the night wore on the action continued, with only a few brief pauses between frenzied blitzes. We must have caught 25 or 30 blackfin before Larry came tight to a fish that took off like a freight train. Scott knew from the blistering run that almost spooled Larry's reel that he had hooked a yellowfin. Twenty minutes later, we heard a shout from the bow as Joe Johnston hooked into a second yellowfin. Would we be lucky enough to land a yellowfin double?

Larry was 45 minutes into the fight and his backing was pointing 200 yards straight down into the gulf. He was about to begin one of the toughest battles in all of fly fishing, lifting a large tuna inch by grueling inch from the depths below. As a general rule, you first feel the pain in your lower back, and as that becomes more intense, your arm muscles start to burn. Depending on your physical condition, the buildup of lactic acid in the muscles can cause you to lose the ability to lift the fish, and when this happens the fight is over. Your only choice is to hand the rod off to someone else. I have heard stories of big yellowfin wearing out an entire crew who took turns on the rod before landing the fish.

An hour into the fight, Larry's face was showing the pain he was feeling in his back and arms. No matter how hard he tried to lift that big tuna, his 12-weight rod didn't budge. I can still vividly picture him bent over the gunwale with his rod stuck underwater up to the stripping guide. Mercifully, the loop in Larry's fly line broke, releasing him and the fish to fight another day. Joe was having an easier time of it, and after a 25-minute battle Lance set the gaff into a 30-pound fish. We had our first yellowfin of the night.

Scott claims that for every 25 blackfin you hook, you usually get one yellowfin. After midnight, we were all starting to fade. Having had only fours hours of sleep in the last 48 hours I was exhausted, but I made the decision to stay up and play the numbers game. It's ironic how your expectations change. Here I was, a confirmed "albieholic," into the next level of tuna fishing—blitzing blackfin—and I was determined to cull as many blackfin as necessary to get a yellowfin. That's how good the tuna fishing can get in the gulf.

Big "Bleeping" Yellowfin!

Around 2 A.M. things started to slow down, or perhaps it was just us. The mate went below to take a nap. Larry was still recovering from his epic battle. The two Joes and I continued to cull through blackfin looking for the elusive yellowfin. At about 2:30, Joe Darcy hooked into a good fish; he thought it might even be a yellowfin. Scott watched the fight intently and was confident that it was just a nice-sized blackfin. The fish's runs weren't the long, screaming runs of a yellowfin.

Joe Darcy's 60-pound yellowfin

Joe skillfully played the fish, and after about 20 minutes he had it to the boat. Scott was up on the flying bridge, and he hollered to Joe Johnston to land the fish. When Joe leaned over the rail to grab the fish, to our shock he screamed, "Yellowfin—a big 'bleeping' yellowfin!" Since landing a big yellowfin was not to be left to a novice, the captain yelled for his mate to come on deck, but Lance was already on his way out of the cabin. Five minutes later he gaffed a 60-pound yellowfin and tossed it onto the deck.

We all congratulated Joe on his awesome tuna. He was jumping up and down, giving everyone high fives and smiling the biggest shit-eating grin I had ever seen. Did he have tuna fever? Well, you tell me—here was a retired New York City electrician with very little sleep in the last 48 hours, in the path of a Category 4 hurricane at three in the morning, acting like a six-year-old kid on Christmas morning. I'd call that tuna fever!

Tuna with Attitude

After we calmed down from the excitement of Joe's catch, I settled in for some more fishing. I desperately wanted to rest my back and arms and take a short nap, but with only a few hours until first light, my window for hooking a yellowfin tuna on this trip was starting to close. So I continued to cull through blackfin in the hope that the law of averages would offer me a yellowfin.

After another half-dozen fish, I stuck my fly into a fish that didn't move. I set the hook again and that really pissed the fish off. This time it took my full fly line and over 200 yards of backing before Scott was able to start the motor and follow the fish with the boat. It was definitely a yellowfin. The only question was whether it was small enough to land on a fly rod.

As I write this, no one on the planet has ever landed a 100-pound yellowfin with a fly rod. While I would love to be the first, there are plenty of reasons why it hasn't happened yet.

I wanted to land this fish so bad that I actually prayed it was well under 100 pounds. As it turned out, I would be doing a lot of praying over the next hour and a half. The first 30 minutes of the fight were typical— the fish making long runs and Scott backing the boat down to allow me to gain back some line. At 45 minutes, I was still in pretty good condition (the months of training at the gym were paying off), but the fish was showing no signs of tiring and I was starting to really worry about its size. Was I hooked to a landable fish?

After an hour, things started to go south. I was completely drenched in sweat, my back felt like it was on fire, and my muscles were starting to burn, although I still had strength in my arms. Both my rod hand and reel hand were beginning to cramp, and I had to force myself to stay positive. Finally, a welcome sign: My fly line was coming back on the reel for the first time. I was gaining on the fish.

My confidence began to build. I really believed the fight was drawing to a close. But we would soon discover that this was a tuna with attitude. With over half my fly line back on the reel and the drag set as tight as I dared, the tuna surged straight down, taking the fly line and 50 yards of backing in seconds and undoing 15 minutes of hard work. The fish stopped, and I again began the slow, tedious, painful process of lifting it to gain line. With each lift up and wind down, I gained about a foot. Eventually, about half the fly line was back on the reel.

To our collective amazement, the tuna took off again. This time, in addition to the drag, I put pressure on the fish by palming the reel. This tuna meant business, though, and for the first time during the battle it headed directly for the rig, which was now only 100 yards behind our boat. I could barely hear Scott, who was screaming over the noise of the boat's engine and the machinery on the rig: "Stop that fish! If he reaches the rig, the fight is over!"

I applied as much side pressure as I could, and it stopped just short of the rig. Scott slid the boat back toward the rig but off to the side, and

I was able to once again get my fly line back on the reel. We actually got below and to the side of the tuna and the rig, which Scott hoped would force the fish to take off away from the pressure, and the rig.

This tactic worked like a charm, and the fish bolted away. I backed off on the drag and let it run a couple hundred yards away. Scott then followed the fish, letting me reel up my backing and put the fly line on the reel for the third time.

This happened a total of 11 times before we got to the end game. Each time I regained my fly line, a new ray of hope; each time the tuna took me into my backing, a new level of fear and frustration. After the seventh or eighth time I lost my fly line, I asked the mate, who had been by my side the entire battle, "Will this fish ever give up?" He looked at me and smiled, saying only, "Eventually." "Before I do?" I inquired. Assessing my condition, he replied, "Yes, if he's less than 100 pounds—over 100 pounds has never been done." Scott joined in, "If this fish isn't over 100 pounds, then it's a fish with one hell of a bad attitude."

Our discussion was rudely interrupted as the tuna, with a fresh burst of speed, streaked toward the surface and the boat's stern. As it flashed by within 20 feet of the boat, we caught a glimpse of what caused its sudden outburst. A 10-foot bull shark was on the tuna's trail. The last thing I wanted was an issue with a shark, although it did put the tuna near the surface and enabled me to gain and keep most of my fly line on

The author's first yellowfin

the reel. Lance lured the shark close to the boat with blackfin tuna chunks and then whacked it on the head with the butt of the gaff. Fortunately we never saw it again.

The tuna stayed close to the boat for the next 10 to 15 minutes, which was a blessing for me. With the strain from the battle, the heat, the humidity, the lights from the rig blurring my vision, and the added heat every few minutes from the flame off the rig, I felt like I was fishing in hell.

After almost an hour and a half, the tuna was nearly done. It began thrashing on the surface, and I could see lights reflecting off its silver sides. Scott backed down on the fish as I kept pressure on it. Lance drove the gaff home on the first try and dropped the 65-pound tuna onto the deck. Unlike Joe Darcy, I wasn't in any condition to celebrate just then. I was just as ecstatic, but I was physically exhausted and relieved—relieved that I had broken my yellowfin curse. I quietly thanked Scott, Lance, and my partners for their help, sat down, and dropped my sweat-drenched head into my hands and mumbled under my breath, "Finally."

The Morning After

It wasn't long before first light treated us to blitzing blackfin and yellowfin surrounding the boat. Joe Darcy and I let Larry and Joe Johnston cast away. It wasn't that we were unselfish; we just didn't want to cast for fear of hooking another big yellowfin. Joe J. landed another yellowfin that weighed about 40 pounds, giving us a total of four for the trip.

Larry hooked another monster yellowfin, and after another epic battle his 14-weight rod broke just below the first ferrule, leaving him with about 2 1/2 feet of graphite. With the now much shorter and stiffer rod, Larry was really able to pressure the fish and rapidly gain line. The fish was almost in sight when it surged under the boat. With the shortened stick, Larry didn't have enough leverage to change the fish's direction, and the leader broke off on the bottom of the boat. We all felt bad for Larry, since he had fought two epic battles only to come up short in the end when his tackle gave in. However, he was the first to sign up for our next trip to Venice.

When the sun was well up and the surface activity was over, we all agreed that it was time to head back. After all, powerful Hurricane Dennis was still on our tail.

On the way back to the docks, we shared our favorite memories of the night. Scott said that with 75 to 80 blackfin and four yellowfin, it was by far his most successful fly trip for tuna. The two biggest yellowfin topped his previous best by over 20 pounds, and he believed they were the third and fourth biggest yellowfin landed on a fly in Louisiana.

All's well that ends well. We beat Dennis to the coast and were able to get over to Palm Beach without any travel delays.

Description

Yellowfin are the most beautiful and brilliantly colored of all tuna. They get their name from their dorsal fins, which are bright yellow. Their body is a metallic dark blue above, their lower sides silvery white, and their belly mostly white. The yellowfin's most dramatic feature is the brilliant golden stripe that runs along its sides. The second dorsal and anal fins are also bright yellow.

They are one of the largest and fastest-growing tuna. Their pectoral fins can reach the base of their second dorsal, but not beyond. And they have small, conical teeth. Even big 200-pound-plus yellowfin tuna can be distinguished from other large species because they appear more slender than bluefin and bigeye tuna, with smaller heads and eyes. But while their eyes may be smaller, yellowfin are believed to have better eyesight than other tuna, and this may account for why they're such prolific nighttime feeders.

Distribution and Behavior

Yellowfin are one of the more tropical species of tuna, preferring water temperatures from 65 to 88 degrees Fahrenheit, with 68 to 72 degrees the optimum. Their range is worldwide in tropical and subtropical seas except for the Mediterranean Sea. On the East Coast they range from southern New England to the Florida Keys and throughout the Gulf of Mexico, and they are usually found in or close to the Gulf Stream.

They like to stay in the thermocline, and the deeper it is, the better they like it. Below the thermocline, the water is colder and there is less oxygen. The thermocline should be viewed by anglers as structure or a barrier; it's a zone in which the water temperature changes more rapidly than in the water above or below it. The thermocline can occur anywhere from about 30 feet to more than 1,000 feet below the surface. Many fish won't swim down through it, and prey and predators often hold just above it.

In the warm tropics, yellowfin tuna may go as deep as 300 feet. In the Northeast, where the deep water is too cold for yellowfin, they usually don't go below 40 feet. They tend to hold deeper in the water column on bright, calm days than on cloudy, rough days.

Yellowfin tuna, like false albacore, have been expanding their range north. Captain Dave Preble, who pioneered fly fishing for yellowfin in the Northeast, reports that in the early 1970s there were no recorded landings of yellowfin at any port in Rhode Island. By the mid-1970s, catches of yellowfin started to become more common in these waters. Not only did catches occur, but they also started to come out of the canyons and closer inshore, and fish showed on the continental shelf as close as the 20-fathom line.

Because yellowfin are very sensitive to temperature changes, global warming seems to be the most likely reason for their expansion northward. They travel and feed in tight schools, usually made up of the same year class. Unlike bluefin tuna, which often hunt cooperatively, yellowfin are competitive predators and often feed in a violent pattern, with surface blitzes, jumping and blasting through bait. Captain Peace Marvel, who owns Reel Peace Charters out of Venice, Louisiana, compares an all-out yellowfin blitz to "a bunch of drunken cowboys running around a whorehouse."

Life History

Like blackfin, yellowfin tuna reach sexual maturity very early in life, some as early as 12 to 15 months. But most are sexually mature at two to three years. They are prolific breeders, spawning several times a year offshore in waters above 78 degrees. Yellowfin grow incredibly fast, weighing as much as 35 pounds at two years of age. In comparison, blackfin weigh 5 or 6 pounds at two years, and bluefin about 20 pounds.

At five years of age a yellowfin can weigh over 175 pounds, while a bluefin might weigh around 100 pounds. Yellowfin are one of the staples of the canning industry, classified as "light tuna." Because of their rapid growth rate and the fact that they reach sexual maturity so early, to date yellowfin appear to have withstood heavy fishing pressure.

Fly Fishing

No sane angler would consider tackling yellowfin tuna on a fly, but this book is not about sanity, it's about extreme fly fishing. And yellowfin tuna certainly fit the bill. While they are an offshore bluewater species found in the deep waters of the Gulf Stream, they will sometimes feed at the surface and can be seen busting bait under birds. When fish aren't visible, the common method to bring them into fly-rod range is to chum or chunk for them. Yellowfin come readily to the surface when they're chummed from a boat and will hit a surface popper.

When hooked, they often go straight down at amazing speeds. Their fight will be long and deep and will test your tackle, strength, and stamina, as well as your will to win. Fly rods of 12- and 14-weight are best suited for this fishery, since they provide the lifting power necessary to pry yellowfin from the depths. Pulling a tuna up feels like digging a trench or a grave—hopefully not your own—and the strongest of backs will eventually succumb to the torture. Even targeting the so-called schoolie yellowfin is not for the faint of heart, and you never know when a real monster is lurking below the chum slick.

Hot Spots

You can find yellowfin tuna in the offshore waters of the Gulf Stream from southern New England to the Florida Keys and throughout the Gulf of Mexico. The three best spots to target yellowfin are the Outer Banks of North Carolina, the waters off Bermuda, and the Gulf of Mexico off the Louisiana coast.

The Outer Banks have always been a yellowfin hot spot. Yellowfin tuna are one of the most abundant fish in the Gulf Stream, which in North Carolina is located about 35 miles southeast of Oregon Inlet and 35 miles east from the Hatteras Inlet. While yellowfin are taken in these waters year-round, large numbers of school-sized fish turn up in the fall off Hatteras shortly before the bluefin arrive. They provide a spectacular fall and early winter fishery.

Bermuda is one of the most overlooked fly-rod destinations. It boasts some of the world's finest yellowfin tuna fishing and has yielded numerous world records, including Jimmy Lopez's early 12- and 16-pound class-tippet records. From Bermuda's west end, it's a short run to the edge of Challenger and Argus Banks, where occasionally the fish are only 15 miles offshore. Prime time is late spring and early summer, when huge numbers of yellowfin tuna are moving through the area. Charters anchor just on the edges of the banks and chum fish into range.

An incredible yellowfin fishery also exists in the Gulf of Mexico. You would be hard pressed to find a better port than Venice from which to launch in southeast Louisiana. From here, there are 1,000-foot-deep tuna hot spots only 20 miles offshore. Winter action for yellowfin tuna and big wahoo on the Midnight Lump is nothing short of phenomenal.

Records

Mark Sosin landed the first recorded yellowfin tuna on a fly in July 1969. His record was broken four years later when Jim Lopez landed an 81-pound fish off Bermuda. From 1973 until 2001, Lopez's record stood as the largest fly-rod yellowfin. For years it was believed that you couldn't land a 100-pound yellowfin on a fly. In the spring of 2001, while writing about fly-rod world records in *False Albacore,* I stated, "Like bluefin, yellowfin weighing over 100 pounds are very difficult to land on a fly, but increasing numbers of fly-rodders are targeting them. You can expect to see an assault on all the class-tippet records in the next few years."

Since then, six fly-rod tippet-class records for yellowfin tuna have been broken. On May 22, 2001, Dr. Richard Sallie landed the first fly-caught tuna over 90 pounds with his 16-pound tippet-class record of 95 pounds 14 ounces shattering the record that stood for almost 30 years. On June 4, 2002, Peter Morse took the 20-pound tippet-class record of 93 pounds 11 ounces. Both fish were caught off the coast of Australia.

One of the most likely spots in the United States for this record to be broken is Venice, Louisiana. Venice is at the mouth of the Mississippi River, and Captain Peace Marvel of Reel Peace Charters claims, "Year-round we are the number-one tuna fishery in North America." Hundred-pound yellowfin tuna caught on conventional gear are brought in to the docks daily in Venice. While Peace's biggest fly-caught yellowfin was 74 pounds, he has hooked many dozens in the 100- to 150-pound range and is confident that it's only a matter of time until one makes it to the boat.

Another area that could set the record is off Key West on the Boca Grand Bar. The bar is southwest of Key West, where the water drops from 120 to 180 feet. Captains anchor on the shallow side of the bar and chum with live pilchards. Yellowfin can be chummed right up to a boat's transom. Getting them to take a fly is not the problem—the challenge is overcoming all the obstacles to landing one. Captain Robbie Delph had a record-breaker on for 45 minutes and then lost his line around a lobster trap. And Robbie's father, Ralph Delph, guided Christian Martin to a fly-rod world-record yellowfin, but it was lost to a shark late in the battle.

The IGFA all-tackle record yellowfin tuna weighed 388 pounds 12 ounces. Curt Wiesenhutter caught it on April 1, 1977, off the Revillagigedo Islands in Mexico.

Current IGFA Fly-Rod Records for Yellowfin Tuna

Tippet	Weight (lbs./oz.)	Location	Angler	Date
Male				
2	3/13	Cross, Seamount, HI	Kevin Nakamaru	4/6/95
4	11/4	Cabo San Lucas, Mexico	Robert Cunningham Jr.	11/21/98
6	34/8	Kandrian, New Guinea	Hitoshi Kira	11/8/03
8	42/5	Maiquetia, Venezuela	A. C. Reuter	1/10/91
12	67/8	Bermuda	Jim Lopez	7/7/73
16	95/14	Carnarvon, Australia	Dr. Richard Sallie	5/22/01
20	93/11	Shark Bay, Western Australia	Peter Morse	6/4/02
Female				
2	Vacant			
4	Vacant			
6	6/8	Baja, Mexico	Donna Anderson	11/29/98
8	15/6	Baja, Mexico	Donna Anderson	11/29/98
12	24/12	Argus Bank, Bermuda	Kathy Williams	6/21/01
16	55/8	Oregon Inlet, NC	Theresa Hutchins	12/5/01
20	53/4	Hatteras Inlet, NC	Sarah M. Gardner	12/6/01

Atlantic Bluefin (*Thunnus thynnus*)

The Beasts of the Bay

For several years, I had been hearing scattered reports of schoolie bluefin tuna being taken by fly-rodders in Cape Cod Bay, as well as the near-shore waters off Cape Cod, Massachusetts. But in the late summer and early fall of 2002, this fishery blew wide open, with almost daily reports of fly-rod bluefin.

Peter McCarthy, one of my fishing partners and a member of Coastal Flyrodders, our local saltwater fly-fishing club, witnessed firsthand this blossoming new fly-rod fishery in early September of that year. Peter landed not one but two bluefin tuna on his half-day charter with Captain Steve Moore. At the next club meeting after his epic trip, Peter, armed with photos of his trophies, filled all 12 spots for his 2003 trip to the cape in a matter of minutes, with many disappointed anglers relegated to a waiting list.

Peter's first bluefin tuna was caught on a "devil stick," our club's nickname for spinning rods. But he landed the second fish on a 12-weight fly rod, which shattered boatside as the captain attempted to gaff the fish. Despite the broken rod, they were still able to land this massive trophy. Photos of Peter with his shattered rod and trophy bluefin graced the pages of all the fly-fishing publications for the next few months and added fuel to our group's burning desire to tangle with these aquatic beasts. We spent the following winter tying big flies on strong hooks, building 12- and 14-weight fly rods, and practicing Bimini knots.

While many of our club members made their annual spring striper trip to Martha's Vineyard, the buzz that summer of 2003 was about our upcoming fall pilgrimage to the cape. The weeks leading up to the trip found us glued to our laptop computers, surfing Northeast fly-fishing Web sites and e-mailing guides for up-to-the-minute bluefin tuna reports. Much to our dismay, the reports of bluefin were few and far between. At the last minute, we all decided to pack our 9- and 10-weight outfits as well, resigned to the fact that we would most likely be chasing striped bass and bluefish.

Peter McCarthy and Captain Steve Moore with bluefin and broken rod

Peter did a first-rate job organizing the trip, booking six veteran bluefin tuna guides. Their strategy was to trailer their boats so that we, like the fish, would be highly mobile. Most of the anglers and guides met for dinner on the eve of our first full day on the water. As we developed our battle plans, we were given a glimmer of hope. One of the guides had heard a report of a few small pods of schoolie bluefin busting bait off Race Point on the tip of the cape. As our evening ended, we planned to meet at 5 A.M. the next morning at the large truck stop just off Interstate 95.

With the excitement and anticipation of what might be ahead of us, no one got much sleep. By 4:30, everyone had assembled at the designated truck stop. After the 20-minute ride to the water, we launched out of a site near Race Point and slowly fanned out into the early fog, looking and listening for any evidence of fish.

Lenny Maiorano and I were teamed up with Captain Jaime Boyle, a veteran guide from Martha's Vineyard that I had fished with several times, although never for bluefin. The morning fog was so thick that visibility was near zero and almost no other boats were on the water, so my fellow anglers and I had Cape Cod Bay practically to ourselves. As the drone of the other boats in our group began to fade, we were left with an almost eerie silence.

After what seemed like an eternity, the quiet was interrupted by the radio blasting news that schools of striped bass had peanut bunker and sand eels pinned against the beach up near the point. Striped bass are a far cry from bluefin, but we decided to give them a shot in order to get the skunk out of our boat.

Following a short ride through the lifting fog, we began to see fish busting as hundreds of bass feasted in a foot of gin-clear water just inches from the beach. At the water's edge, the beach was twinkling with flashes of sand eels and peanut bunker flapping on the sand. The baitfish had beached themselves in order to avoid their certain fate in the jaws of hungry striped bass. From 60 feet away with our 9- and 10-weight rods, we tossed Clouser Minnows up onto the sand and slowly stripped them back. As soon as our flies reached the water, we were tight to bass. This warmup was great fun for a while, but we were eager to bring out our big guns and find some bluefin tuna.

The radio suddenly blared again as one of our boats reported that it was heading toward a big push of fish in the middle of the bay. Armed with the same message, we could hear the roar of the other dormant boats in our group start their engines and begin to race toward the lead boat with great anticipation. When we got within 100 yards of the action, we could see that the first boat on the scene had hooked up.

After cutting the motor, we drifted toward the mêlée in anticipation of bluefin tuna. As the roar of our engine faded, we got the news—we were into bluefish, acres of them. Not the cocktail-sized blues I had been catching all summer back home in New Jersey, but jumbo blues weighing in the midteens.

On any other day I would have been jumping out of my skin at the thought of taking big blues on the surface. But we were targeting bluefin, and we were burning daylight. Reluctantly, Lenny and I decided to take advantage of what Mother Nature was offering. We quickly put wire on the patterns we had used for the bass and were both tight to monster blues as soon as the flies hit water. We were summarily entertained by their long, powerful runs and gill-rattling jumps. I had forgotten just how tough big bluefish can be. After 10-minute battles, the two jumbos were finally caught and released.

We debated whether to cast again. After all, how many times a season are you surrounded by hungry monster blues? Then we heard another blast from the radio. From the elevated pitch of Captain Terry Nugent's voice, we knew even before the words were formed that he had hit pay dirt. "Bluefin—'bleeping,' 'bleeping' bluefin on top!" Terry exclaimed. "Three pods on top, blasting the 'bleeping' hell out of the bait!"

We could hear jubilant shouts from all the boats in our party as they ripped through Cape Cod Bay in Terry's direction. The sun was begin-

STEVE MOORE

Blitzing bluefin attract seabirds.

ning to burn off the last of the morning fog and soon we were able to see Terry's boat, *Rip Tide,* surrounded by bluefin tuna churning the water white with foam. I had never seen a school of fish throw so much water. At first it looked like a stampeding herd of wild horses racing through shallow water.

What came next gave us all a bad case of buck fever: Bluefin tuna in the 50- to 100-pound range were porpoising through bait sprays with mouths wide open, churning up the helpless prey. Several fish completely cleared the water, showing us their full length and power, as if to say, "Hey, buddy, do you really want to tangle with me?"

These Fish Can Make a Grown Man Cry

Jaime positioned his boat, the *Boylermaker,* perfectly for our first shot at these massive creatures. As he cut the engine we were 200 feet in front of the school, and they were closing fast. Lenny and I were armed with 12-weight rods and large tinker mackerel patterns tied by master tier Dave Skok. When the fish were within 100 feet, we tossed our offerings directly into their path. Within seconds, bluefin were boiling on, but refusing, our flies. The last fish boiled on my offering within 30 feet of the boat as I made the retrieve.

As the fish continued to spray bait, we could see that they were feeding on tiny peanut bunker. The problem was that our flies were too big. I quickly pulled a few small peanut bunker patterns from my boat bag, but my hands were shaking so badly I couldn't tie them on. Jaime, observing my predicament, took a fly and swiftly tied it to my tippet, but by then the fish were gone. He saw my disappointment and said, "These fish can make a grown man cry." The bluefin showed only a few more times, and we didn't get another good shot before we had to head to the docks.

Back on dry land we relaxed over a few beers and recounted our day. We all admitted that we enjoyed sight fishing for bass in a foot of water and casting to acres of alligator bluefish. While no one had hooked a bluefin, one by one we described the thrill of our close encounters with the "beasts of the bay." That evening, we tied peanut bunker patterns, resharpened our hooks, and tied fresh leaders onto our fly lines in preparation for the next day's skirmishes.

Hero or Zero

Lenny and I drew Captain Terry Nugent for our second day of fishing. (Terry's day job is serving as a Massachusetts state policeman.) He has a reputation for being a bit of a cowboy, and he's famous for the amount of water he covers and the speed with which he covers it during the course of a day's fishing.

There was a good chop on the water that morning, but Terry was determined to be the first boat on fish. He put the pedal to the metal, and as we rushed past the other boats in our group, he advised us to hold on tight because it might be a little bumpy. "A little bumpy" was the understatement of the trip. I have never had the opportunity, or for that matter the desire, to ride a bucking bronco, but I think I got very close to experiencing the thrill and the agony of it on our run across the bay that morning. Terry's favorite expression is, "In this game, you're either a hero or a zero," and we were determined to have the group end the day as heroes.

While Terry throws caution to the wind in getting to the fish, once he finds them he has an uncanny ability to predict their behavior and get his anglers into position. Although there were only a few small pods of bluefin working, time and again Terry would get us in front of a pod, and it wasn't long before we started getting legitimate fly-rod shots.

When a larger school surfaced 200 yards away, Terry quickly got into position in front of them and cut the motor, giving us a perfect drift. Having already blown several shots, Lenny and I were more patient this time and waited until the fish were in range. Finally we were able to present our flies right in front of the churning school.

On my second strip I was tight to a tuna and my line started melting off the screaming reel. The first run was approximately 200 yards in less than 20 seconds. Even though my reel contained 500 yards of backing, Terry started the motor and began to chase the fish, explaining that we were less than a quarter mile from the high flyers. (High flyers are poles with flags that mark lobster pots, and they are connected to the pots via heavy ropes, an angler's worst nightmare.) Several times we closed the gap on the tuna and got most of the backing on the reel, only to have the fish rip off another 50 to 100 yards.

After three or four scorching runs, the fish sounded deep. This changed the angle of the fight from horizontal to vertical. I was glad I'd opted for my 14-weight rod and not the lighter 12-weight that I'd used the day before. With the lifting power of the heavier rod, I felt the battle would eventually turn in my favor. By putting the rod tip in the water, lifting with all my power to move the rod up to about 45 degrees above the water, and then winding down until the tip was back in the water, I was able to slowly gain line, about a foot on each lift.

It was about 25 minutes into the fight when I got the fly line back to the reel. This was a great relief. Not only was the fish getting closer, but there was now one less knot to fail. The line I was using was specifically designed for chasing big bluewater species. It was stronger and longer than standard lines. It had a 50-pound core and was 150 feet long, which would enable me to spend more time fighting the fish with the fly line instead of the backing. Despite the increasing burning sensation in my biceps and forearms, with Terry's calm coaching I was gaining confidence on every lift.

That all changed in an instant when Terry suddenly throttled down on the engine and started barking instructions over the roar of the motor. Out of the corner of my eye I saw what had spooked him. We were drifting into those damn high flyers. After all the time and effort, what a sorry way this would be to lose the fish, wrapped around a lobster-pot rope.

Terry skillfully positioned the boat directly over the fish so the line was straight down. Then Lenny jumped up on the bow, peered into the water, and told us which way he thought we should pressure the fish. Lenny's call was right on the money, and we drifted past the high flyer with my line and the tuna coming within a foot of the rope.

The Twelfth and Final Round

Around an hour into the fight things were going well, but fatigue was starting to take its toll—on the fish and the angler. Between the strength of this powerful fish and the heat of the sun beating down on me, I was starting to fade. My clothes were drenched with sweat, and my mouth was so dry I could barely talk.

Fortunately, Lenny realized my plight and again came to the rescue. He squirted refreshingly ice-cold water from a plastic bottle into my mouth and poured the remaining water over the top of my head. I felt like a heavyweight fighter who had just finished the eleventh round: beat up and bloody, but ahead on points. All I needed to do was answer the bell and finish the twelfth round standing, and the victory was mine.

A sudden surge from the tuna signaled that the final round was on. Buoyed by the brief jolt of energy from the water break, I started to close the distance between the tuna and our boat. After all, my opponent didn't have help in his corner. We were approximately an hour and 15 minutes into the fight when we reached another milestone. I got the back end of the 24-foot sink tip of the fly line on the reel and saw a flash of silver as the sun bounced off the tuna's metallic side.

The author with a bluefin tuna going deep into the backing.

Terry got on the radio and hollered, "We've got color," signaling the fight was coming to an end. The fish was in the final stages of its death spiral, just out of gaff range below the boat. Terry could clearly see the tuna and confirmed that we had a big fish, which he estimated to be in the 80- to 85-pound range. This would be my biggest fly-rod tuna to date. I hadn't noticed before, but the other five boats in our party had come over to photo-document the battle and congratulate me on my trophy. Remembering Terry's words, I was determined to be the hero, not the zero.

The Agony of Defeat

For the next 15 minutes, the fish and I fought over where the 24-foot shooting head should be. I wanted it well on the reel and the fish wanted it deep in the water column. As I was about to get it back on the reel for the fourth time, Terry readied the gaff. I said to myself, "Now is the time for me to finish this battle."

The guide was ready, I was ready, and I thought the fish was ready to surrender. I leaned back on the rod as I had done a hundred times before during the past hour and a half. Then the unthinkable happened. In less than a heartbeat I was lying flat on the deck with loose line dangling on my chest. I just laid there with a sinking feeling of failure rushing through my veins. The thrill of victory had been so close.

I was frantic to find out what went wrong. Did I pull too hard and break the tippet? Did my loop knot to the fly slip? Or had my Bimini loop to the butt of the leader failed? In my haste, did I make the whipped loop on the front of the fly line too short? Terry finally determined that it wasn't angler error. It was, in fact, the specially designed big-game fly line that had failed me. It parted exactly where the manufacturer fused the running line to the sink tip.

We were relieved to know that we had carried out our part of the conquest without a major mistake. I would later find out that during the season, three other bluefin tuna were lost boatside for the same reason with the same fly line. It was small comfort, but at least I knew I would relish the ensuing war of words in my correspondence with the manufacturer upon my return home. "And no, thank you, I don't want a complimentary replacement line!"

Later that day we heard that the *Boylermaker* was tight. We were still chasing a few small pods of tuna when I hooked a second fish, which like the first raced off 200 yards of backing in seconds. Unfortunately, it headed directly in front of a troller's path. We hollered and waved but couldn't get their attention, and their motor cut my backing. I had mixed feelings about the cutoff. On one hand, I would've loved to have landed one of these magnificent creatures that day, but on the other, I questioned whether I was physically up to another contest.

The sparse pods of bluefin soon disappeared, so we headed over to the *Boylermaker* and discovered that Pete Douma was now an hour and a half into his fight with his first bluefin. It was getting very hot, and as we approached I could see the agony on Pete's face. I also could imagine the pain he was experiencing in his arms and back. Pete and his fish were fighting an epic battle, and they were both totally fatigued. I picked up my camera to document the impending catch, although I felt guilty taking pictures of the two warriors now locked in a standoff. The fish weakly swam in a tight death spiral. Pete tried desperately to close the gap between them. His partner, Ed Janiga, was poised and ready with the gaff.

After another hour, the captain and Pete realized it was a hopeless standoff. Pete somewhat dejectedly handed his 12-weight rod over to Ed to close out the battle. With a fresh set of arms, Ed was able to move the defeated fish into position and Jaime drove the gaff into the side of the fish, lifted it over the gunwale, and dropped it on the deck. As the word spread, you could hear shouts of joy and relief coming from the other boats all over the bay. Our group had reached its goal of landing a bluefin tuna on a fly.

Captain Jaime Boyle and Pete Douma show off a schoolie bluefin.

At the end of three days of fishing, the total bluefin tuna score for 12 anglers and 6 guides was 5 fish hooked, 2 landed, 1 rod shattered, and 3 fly lines destroyed. But these numbers don't begin to do the trip justice. The dinner party on the final evening was filled with smiles, cheers, and congratulations. When Peter McCarthy asked if anyone wanted to try again next year, all 12 anglers' hands were held high.

After this trip, besides finding a reliable fly line, I decided to go on a major diet and join a gym. I was determined to be ready for the physical challenge of fly fishing for bluefin tuna the next year. As outdoor writer Nick Curcione likes to say, "There is no such thing as an out-of-shape tuna."

Description

Giants. That's what mature bluefin tuna are called, and giants they are in every sense of the word. They are giants when it comes to speed, strength, and stamina, and they are the largest of our finfish. The National Marine Fisheries Service (NMFS) considers bluefin "giants" when they reach a curved fork length of 81 inches; a fish of that length would weigh over 300 pounds. This happens at about the time they reach sexual maturity, which is between 7 and 11 years of age.

Also, in Japan's fish market they command a giant price. The late author Steve Sloan, in his great book *Ocean Bankruptcy: World Fisheries on the Brink of Disaster*, writes of a 400-pound bluefin tuna being sold in 2001 at a Tokyo auction for $172,000. That's $430 a pound!

"Mediums" are fish measuring between 59 and 73 inches, and these fish would weigh from 135 to 310 pounds. The schoolies that we target with fly rods run from about 27 to 59 inches and weigh between 15 and 135 pounds.

The easiest way to distinguish bluefin from other tuna is by their relatively short pectoral fins, which never reach back as far as the second dorsal. The height of their second dorsal is greater than that of the first dorsal. Their back and upper sides are deep metallic blue. Their lower sides and belly are white, with somewhat colorless lines and rows of dots. And the finlets are yellow and edged in black.

Distribution and Behavior

Atlantic bluefin are great wanderers and are widely distributed throughout the Atlantic Ocean. They often make incredibly long migrations and occur in tropical, subtropical, and temperate waters of the world's oceans, preferring water temperatures in the 50- to 82-degree Fahrenheit range. In the western Atlantic they travel as far north as Labrador and Newfoundland and as far south as Brazil. Bluefin can maintain a higher body temperature than any other tuna—as high as 35 degrees above the surrounding water temperatures. This allows them to move into the cold Canadian waters in search of prey.

They hunt cooperatively, as do some other highly advanced predators such as killer whales and wolves. Bluefin are primarily an offshore fish, but they do venture farther inshore than yellowfin, albacore, and bigeye tuna. There have even been a few reports of bluefin being taken from shore on spinning tackle. I have seen many taken within sight of land, sometimes only a few hundred yards off the beach.

Life History

Bluefin tuna grow larger and can live longer than any other tuna species. They can grow up to 15 feet, weigh up to 1,500 pounds, and live for 25 to 40 years. They don't reach sexual maturity until at least seven years of age and 300 pounds. Bluefin are the latest of all tuna species to reach sexual maturity.

A dragger culls through its catch.

Throughout the world, many bluefin tuna are removed from our oceans before they have a chance to spawn. We can't maintain a sustainable population if they aren't allowed to reach sexual maturity and reproduce. Current research indicates that Atlantic bluefin tuna spawn in two locations, the Gulf of Mexico and the Mediterranean Sea. Spawning occurs in the gulf between May and June and in the Mediterranean and Adriatic seas from June through August.

Fly Fishing

Catching a bluefin on a fly can be a Herculean task. Just finding one smaller than a VW Beetle is problematic. If you do decide to come over to the dark side of fly fishing—pursuing bluefin tuna is an extreme sport if there ever was one—be prepared for crushed tackle and bruised egos.

As evidenced by Peter's shattered 12-weight fly rod and my busted bluewater fly line in the opening story of this chapter, bluefin tuna are extremely difficult to catch on a fly rod. Because of their great size, strength, and speed, your tackle must be top-notch. Rods of at least 12- to 14-weight with plenty of lifting power are required to power these fish back to the boat. You will need a reel with a smooth, strong drag and large capacity for a fly line and a minimum of 400 yards of backing.

Hot Spots

In New England you can target bluefin tuna out of Gloucester and Cape Ann, Cape Cod and off the Vineyard, and from Nantucket, Massachusetts. Cape Cod Bay has had a very good bite of schoolie bluefin tuna, as has Stellwagen Bank, which lies 14 miles off Gloucester and just 5½ miles off Race Point on the cape.

In Rhode Island, Point Judith has a large charter fleet that targets tuna. From August into early October, schoolie bluefin tuna come into an area known as the Mud Hole, which is southeast of Block Island. When the draggers are working this area, the fly fishing can be spectacular. They drag all night and cull their bycatch in the morning. The tuna have figured out that this provides an easy meal.

In New York, the Butterfish Hole, which lies about 15 miles south-southwest of Montauk Point, is a renowned tuna hot spot, especially in the fall. In New Jersey, bluefin show up at another area named the Mud Hole around the middle of June, and they are available through November. During these months, they are also found well offshore in the Hudson and Wilmington canyons.

While I'm certain that 100-pound bluefin have been taken in New England on the fly, if you're looking for a fly-rod world-record bluefin, North Carolina's Outer Banks is the place to go. I personally know of six 100-pound fly-caught bluefin tuna taken off the coast of North Carolina, all between Cape Hatteras and Cape Lookout. Bluefin start showing up in late autumn and can stay into April, but January through March is prime time.

Fly fishing for bluefin is still in its infancy, with four of the five male fly-rod class-tippet records taken after 1995 and all three female tippet-class records taken in 2005.

Records

Ken Frazer took the IGFA all-tackle record of 1,496 pounds off Nova Scotia, Canada, on October 26, 1979.

I would be remiss if I failed to recognize Michael Reid, who landed a 128-pound Hatteras bluefin on January 23, 1996. This catch was the first fly-rod tuna over 100 pounds and stood as the world record until Stephen Hutchins bested it on February 24, 2000, with his then-record 129-pound bluefin, also landed off Hatteras. (See chapter 11 for a detailed account of the current 16- and 20-pound class-tippet records.)

SANDY NOYES

Gail Greenwood-Noyes with one of her three IGFA tippet-class world-record bluefins

Current IGFA Fly-Rod Records for Bluefin

Tippet	Weight (lbs./oz.)	Location	Angler	Date
Male				
2	Vacant			
4	Vacant			
6	14/0	Montauk, NY	Stephen Sloan	8/30/81
8	28/8	Indian River, DE	Rich Winnor	8/7/97
12	42/8	Virginia Beach, VA	David M. Limroth	7/20/97
16	101/8	Hatteras, NC	Raz Reid	2/22/96
20	196/9	Morehead City, NC	Bradley Kistler	1/12/01
Female				
2	Vacant			
4	Vacant			
6	Vacant			
8	Vacant			
12	21/0	Fishers Island, NY	Gail Greenwood-Noyes	7/28/05
16	18/0	Fishers Island, NY	Gail Greenwood-Noyes	7/28/05
20	19/0	Fishers Island, NY	Gail Greenwood-Noyes	7/26/05

Related Species

5

Flyrodding for any member of the tuna family is a tremendously challenging sport. Pound for pound, tuna fight with more strength and endurance than any other fish in the world. We've already covered fly fishing for blackfin, yellowfin, and bluefin tuna. In the pages that follow, you'll find a brief synopsis of the status of fly fishing for the other five species of tuna found in the western Atlantic and the Gulf of Mexico.

False Albacore (*Euthynnus alletteratus*)

Historically, false albacore have been the Rodney Dangerfield of tuna fishing. Not only didn't they get much respect, but in many areas even today they're still used for chum to attract "more desirable" species of tuna. You don't need a permit to fish for them and there are no limits on their harvest, and because of their poor food quality they're rarely harvested commercially. Therefore, they are the most abundant tuna in our oceans. They are a great game fish, and their recreational value has added millions of dollars to many coastal towns' economies.

In the last decade, false albacore have earned the respect of the fly-fishing community. Captain Dave Preble summed it up best when he stated, "False albacore were created in the master design of the universe for fly-rodders. If ever a saltwater fish was made for fly fishing, albies are it."

Although a pelagic species, they seasonally come inshore and are one of the few tuna that you can consistently catch from shore. They are ferocious feeders but can be selective as hell, and no other small inshore

TOM GILMORE

False albacore and fly rods are a perfect match.

fish can match their speed, strength, and stamina. Because of this, it is not surprising that in many areas of the country these fish have developed a cultlike following of anglers.

A Hanging in the Alley

"Albie Alley" might be the best place on the planet to fly fish for tuna from shore. Stretching from the entrance to Edgartown Harbor on Martha's Vineyard to Cape Poge Lighthouse on the northeast corner of Chappaquiddick Island, the alley can be counted on to provide wading anglers daily shots at tuna.

My favorite spot is Cape Poge Gut, which the locals feel is the true Albie Alley on Chappaquiddick Island. This is a narrow opening through which all the bait and predators entering or leaving the waters of Cape Poge Bay must pass through. The gut is only 100 yards wide, and both rising and falling water bring predators very close to shore. You need a four-wheel-drive vehicle and a permit to fish the East Beach side of the alley. Most anglers fish below the bluffs on the North Neck of "Chappy" on a rising tide. On incoming water, the rip sets up close to the bluff side of the gut and brings blitzing false albacore within fly-rod casting range.

This rip was the scene of the "hanging in the alley," according to local guide Kenny Vanderlaske. Kenny and his wife, Lori, are well respected

Vineyard shore guides, each with over two decades of experience. (Lori holds the women's fly-rod record for bluefish with a whopping 18-pound 11-ounce fish.)

As the story goes, the day of the hanging started out like any other day on the Vineyard during albie season. It was a perfect morning, with light winds and a strong full-moon tide pushing into the alley. Cars lined up to catch the "On Time" ferry from Edgartown to Chappaquiddick Island. Once on the island, some anglers stopped to fish the beach at "Chappy" Point while others continued on to the alley.

Once there, anglers waded out to the edge of the deep drop-off and started blind casting into the rip that had formed. It wasn't long before the action busted wide open, with albies crashing on bait and rods arching and reels screaming. The anglers that hooked up did the "albie shuffle," working their way past the picket line of anglers as the fish ran with the tide back into Cape Poge Bay.

One of the novice anglers that Kenny was guiding hooked up on what would have been his first false albacore. As the angler tried to clear his fly line to the reel, the line ripped out of his hand and started jumping wildly from his stripping basket. The line was flying everywhere, and eventually it looped up and over his head. As the albie raced toward the bay, the loop tightened around the stunned angler's neck. To make matters worse, while trying to remove the noose he stumbled and fell head-first into the water.

After a few frantic seconds of being tugged by the albie down-current, the angler was rescued from the drink by his able guide. Cold, soaked, embarrassed, and disappointed that he'd lost the battle with his first false albacore, the fisherman at least could revel in the fact that he survived the hanging in the alley.

Description

False albacore are frequently confused with their inshore cousin, the Atlantic bonito (*Sarda sarda*). While similarly shaped, bonito are only a little more than half the size of false albacore, and their markings are different. Bonito have fairly straight horizontal stripes on their back, with dark vertical patches on their sides. False albacore have a blue-green back with horizontal, irregular, mackerel-type markings and chrome sides and white belly. The most distinguishing markings on false albacore are the three to five dark spots that look like fingerprints between the pectoral and ventral fins on an otherwise all-white belly.

The most definitive way to tell these two fish apart is to throw them on the grill—the one even your cat won't eat is the false albacore. It's a little rough on the fish, but it's a foolproof test. Bonito, on the other hand, are delicious, certainly one of the best-tasting fish I've ever eaten.

Distribution

False albacore swim in the upper waters of the Gulf Stream, making seasonal pilgrimages inshore to feed on large concentrations of prey species. While I'm not aware of any studies of the false albacore's migratory patterns, I suspect that they migrate both north-south in the Gulf Stream as well as east-west to and from the Gulf Stream to feed inshore.

In the Northeast they appear in late August or early September, peaking sometime between mid-September and mid-October, depending on water temperature and the availability of prey species. In North Carolina they usually arrive inshore in early October and stay into mid-December, with peak fishing often occurring around the first two weeks in November.

For years, anglers assumed that New England false albacore moved south to the Outer Banks as the water cooled in the north, but no one could explain the tremendous difference in size between the New England and the North Carolina fish. The New England fish usually run under 10 pounds, with an occasional 12- to 14-pounder in the mix. In

Captain Steve Bellefleur ready to release a false albacore

TOM GILMORE

North Carolina the fish average 10 to 12 pounds, and catching one over 15 pounds is a daily possibility.

In the mid-1990s I started chasing false albacore off the east coast of Florida in the Palm Beach area, where the Gulf Stream is closer to shore than anywhere in North America. The fish arrive there in the spring and peak in June and July, before thinning out and heading northward with the Gulf Stream in August and September. Their size matches that of the North Carolina fish.

I've come to the conclusion that when the New England fish leave for warmer water, most move south and offshore to the Gulf Stream, while most of the fall run in North Carolina includes resident offshore fish and fish from Florida. The largest fly-rod fish annually come from the east coast of Florida and the Outer Banks, the two areas closest to the Gulf Stream. By all accounts, North Carolina, Florida, and the Gulf of Mexico have offshore year-round resident false albacore.

Life History

As a tuna with little or no commercial value, false albacore are last in line when it comes to research dollars. Therefore, very little is known about their migratory patterns, life history, and reproductive biology. It is believed that they reach sexual maturity at approximately 15 inches—roughly two years of age—and spawn offshore sometime between April and November. This would indicate that the fish we're targeting with fly rods have spawned several times before they're caught and, hopefully, released.

Fly Fishing

As I mentioned earlier, false albacore will come close to shore, giving "sand people," as Captain Brian Horsley refers to shore-bound anglers, good opportunities to catch tuna. The best shore areas for tuna are ones that tend to concentrate bait, such as jetties, points, and inlets.

My good friend and fishing partner Ed Janiga has had multiple-fish days from such shore hot spots as Sandy Hook in New Jersey, Shinnecock Inlet in Long Island, and Weekapaug and Quonochontaug breachways in Rhode Island. Ed attributes his success to paying careful attention to details such as tides, moon phases, and bait on an annual basis and using this information to plan his future tuna trips. Once on location, Ed feels it's important to stay put and wait out an entire tide, similar to a deer hunter sitting in a deer stand for most of the day. Patience is the key.

Master fly tier Dave Skok, who has taken more shore albies than anyone I know, agrees with Ed and adds, "It's important to keep your fly in the water." Dave claims that he takes more than half his albies while blind casting. His name appears regularly on the Martha's Vineyard Fishing Derby leader board, and he has won the fly-caught false albacore division several times. In 2001, he took the overall prize for the derby. With these credentials, I'd say Dave's advice is worth paying attention to.

False albacore have little in the way of teeth, so they must take their prey whole. Flies should be relatively small to match the local prey species and tied on sharp, strong hooks. A 9- or 10-weight fly rod should be plenty big enough in the Northeast. For North Carolina and Florida, where the fish tend to run a little larger, I'd suggest a 10- or 11-weight outfit. Reels should have smooth drag systems and the capacity to hold a minimum of 150 yards of 30-pound backing.

As for lines, when possible I like to catch false albacore as they are blitzing on top, and in these situations a clear intermediate line works well. I always have a sinking line of 300 to 350 grains to use when albies are not showing on top or when I'm fishing in strong currents. For leaders and tippets, I have gone exclusively to fluorocarbon, and I'll use as strong a test as the albies will allow. These are tough fish and they will fight to the death if you let them. By using 16- or 20-pound test, you can shorten the fight and give the fish a better chance to survive.

Hot Spots

The bigger false albacore come from down south, off North Carolina and Florida. While Florida holds most of the tippet-class world records, I know of many false albacore caught and released off Harkers Island, North Carolina, that would have set new class-tippet records. If you pressed me for my three top false albacore hot spots for wade fishing, I'd have to say the inlets and breachways on Martha's Vineyard, the south shore of Rhode Island, and Cape Lookout in North Carolina. But almost any major inlet or point from the south side of Cape Cod and the islands in Massachusetts south to Island Beach State Park in New Jersey will give you good shore shots at false albacore.

If you plan to charter a boat for false albacore, there simply is not a place on the face of the planet that compares with the summer run of false albacore off Palm Beach, Florida. I have been fishing this area for over 10 years, and from early June through the end of July you couldn't ask for better conditions or better fishing. Out of perhaps 50 days of fishing, only once did weather prevent us from getting out, and year in and year out the number and size of false albacore are spectacular.

The other two choices from a boat would have to be the fall runs at Harkers Island, North Carolina, and Montauk, New York. The fantastic fall run of false albacore off Montauk Point often occurs alongside blitzing striped bass and bluefish, and it's quite common to land all three on one outing—a Northeast grand slam.

Records

For records, the best spot in the world is Saly, Senegal, which holds six line-class records, five of them going to female angler Odile Robelin, all taken June 9–16, 2000. These record fish range from a pesky little 23-pound 2-ounce fish to a robust 26-pound 7-ounce monster. The world record false albacore is a 35-pound 2-ounce fish taken in Cap de Garde, Algeria, on December 14, 1988, by Jean Yves Chatard.

As for the best spot in North America for large false albacore, the records speak for themselves. Eleven of the 13 tippet-class records come from Florida, with North Carolina and New Jersey accounting for the other two.

Current IGFA Fly-Rod Records for False Albacore

Tippet	Weight (lbs./oz.)	Location	Angler	Date
Male				
2	7/9	Bayhead, NJ	Ron Mazzarella	10/20/01
4	13/8	Key West, FL	Robert Bass	7/23/83
6	18/4	Cape Canaveral, FL	Dave Chermanski	7/24/72
8	17/8	Jupiter, FL	Andy Mill	7/7/96
12	17/12	Key West, FL	Luis de Hoyos	5/18/83
16	19/5	Cape Lookout, NC	Jim Rivers	11/9/00
20	19/0	Dry Tortugas, FL	Philip Caputo	4/12/95
Female				
2	Vacant			
4	5/4	Islamorada, FL	Diane Harbaugh	7/15/03
6	14/4	Key West, FL	Pamela Marmin	4/22/01
8	14/0	Key West, FL	Lisa Booth	5/2/00
12	15/4	Key West, FL	Jennifer Andreae	5/13/99
16	14/13	Key West, FL	Linda Gracie	4/29/00
20	15/8	Port Canaveral, FL	Christine Perez	8/17/00

Atlantic Bonito (*Sarda sarda*)

Gaff, Gut, and Release

An Atlantic bonito was the first species of tuna I landed on a fly, although I really never got a chance to see it. It was early August, and Steve Murphy and I were fishing off the south shore of Rhode Island with Captain Steve Bellefleur. We had each taken several small bass and blues, and the tide was starting to go slack at the tail end of the ebb tide. Captain Steve asked if we would like to run east and see if we could find some bonito to round out a grand slam. He said that a few sightings had been reported, but to date he hadn't heard of any bonito being landed that year.

We were game, and Steve headed his 19-foot Mako east toward Charlestown Breachway at a pretty good clip. About halfway there, he pulled back the throttle as two boats approached us from the east. It turned out they were locals that Steve knew. They had been up at Charlestown for the entire dropping tide looking for bonito, but reported it was dead. Steve thanked them for saving him some serious gas money and as they motored off he opened the cooler, grabbed a sandwich and a cold drink, and said, "We'll just hang out here for a few minutes."

Murphy and I were disappointed by the news that we wouldn't be getting a shot at a grand slam, but we'd had a good morning on bass and bluefish. After the locals were out of sight, Steve started the motor and continued east. He winked at us and quietly said, "Bonito show up at Charlestown on the incoming tide." By the time we got to the breachway, the tide was already coming in.

Steve cut the motor and started scanning for fish. We weren't there five minutes when bonito began popping up here and there. This was the first time I had fished with Steve, and I was beginning to think he was pretty damn good at his job. Since then, Steve has guided me to tons of bonito and false albacore, but that first bonito is still my most memorable catch.

I don't have a picture of it, but the events of that afternoon are still deeply etched in my mind. After about an hour of incoming tide, we had several small pods of bonito working, and Steve was doing a great job of positioning the boat to allow us good shots at the fish. Murphy and I had never seen tuna busting on bait, and at first it really rattled our nerves.

On the first half-dozen or so shots we committed every conceivable angling error, but Steve was patient with us and it paid off. I finally got my fly in front of a few boiling bonito and my line went tight on the first strip. My fly line and backing melted off the small Scientific Anglers reel at a speed that I'd never experienced. Backing that had never seen the light of day was ripping through my fly rod toward Block Island.

Steve warned me that my line might go slack, noting that bonito change direction several times during a fight. If this happened, he instructed, "Reel like hell." A few seconds after his warning, my line went dead and my heart almost stopped. I was certain I had lost the fish, but as instructed I began reeling as fast as I could. I reeled slack line for what seemed an eternity, and I watched my backing sink slowly below the boat. Dejected, I hollered over to Steve, "I lost him!" Steve screamed back, "Reel, damn it, reel!"

As I started to reel again, I saw the line below the boat start tightening in a large circle, and all of a sudden I was tight to the fish. After two shorter runs, the fish was circling below the boat and I was gaining line— the bonito would soon be mine. I was so focused on fighting the fish that I hadn't noticed Steve pick up a gaff. Suddenly, he grabbed my leader, drove the gaff into the bonito, and hoisted it over the gunwale.

As I turned to look for my camera, Steve grabbed his knife and quickly bled the bonito, then shoved it into the water to rinse it off. What happened next would continue to haunt Steve for years. With a final breath, the bonito gave one last kick, slipped through Steve's wet hand, and sank out of sight down to the bottom of Block Island Sound. At first, I didn't know why Steve was pounding the side of the boat and using curse words that I hadn't heard since high school.

When he stood up and turned around, I saw that his hands were empty. He looked at me standing there with my camera in hand and apologized profusely. He said, "Thank God it wasn't your first." He realized instantly from my silence and the look on my face that it had in fact been my first—and you never forget your first!

Steve kept us out late that day, busting his butt to get us some more shots at bonito. He more than did his part, but his anglers weren't up to the challenge. I knew at the end of that day that I would look forward to spending years chasing tuna with Steve. Over the next 15 years, I realized that my first impression of "pretty damn good" was quite an understatement of Steve's guiding abilities.

The next time I fished with Steve after the bonito disaster, I was joined by my good friend and noted author and casting instructor Ed Jaworowski. Ed and I were two of the founders of the Main Line Fly

Tiers in Pennsylvania, and we have fished together for over 30 years. Needless to say, I have learned volumes about fishing from my friendship with Ed.

Steve had us into fish all day long on this trip. Ed and I both landed several bonito and false albacore, as well as a few bass and bluefish. While I generally release most of my fish, Steve kept one bonito to take home, as they are his wife's favorite. We capped off a perfect day when Steve and Susan joined us for dinner at a local restaurant Steve recommended. We celebrated our good luck with a few bottles of chardonnay from a local vineyard and a surprise dinner of our freshly caught bonito, which Steve had arranged with the chef.

Description

Atlantic bonito are one of the most beautiful fish that swim in our oceans. In fact, in Spanish *bonito* means "beautiful." They are generally smaller than their inshore cousins, false albacore. Bonito average 3 to 6 pounds, with a 9- or 10-pound fish a real trophy.

They can be distinguished by the series of seven or more dark, wavy horizontal lines on the upper half of their back, compared to the dark, jagged, mackerel-like markings on the upper back of false albacore. Their back is blue-green and their belly silver to whitish. Bonito have very short pectoral fins and their dorsal fins are long, low, and not di-

TOM GILMORE

The author with a bonito

TOM GILMORE

The bonito's wavy horizontal lines distinguish it from the false albacore's jagged, mackerel-like markings.

vided. False albacore, which bonito are often confused with, have a higher dorsal fin and the base only runs a short distance on their back. Bonito lack the definitive belly spots, or fingerprints, of false albacore. Skipjack have stripes on their belly instead of the back.

As I mentioned before, bonito make great table fare.

Distribution

Bonito are found in the tropical and temperate waters of the Atlantic Ocean from Nova Scotia to Argentina, and they are rare migrants into the Gulf of Mexico. They spend most of their time feeding 15 to 20 miles offshore, and like false albacore, bonito are unusual for tuna in that they often come inshore and even into inlets, bays, and estuaries. This gives the wading angler an opportunity to land an offshore species from shore.

Bonito are more tolerant of cool water than false albacore are, so they arrive inshore earlier and stay longer. In the Northeast, bonito arrive first in the waters around Nantucket and Martha's Vineyard in late July, when the waters warm into the mid-60s. They come in from the Gulf Stream on plumes that break off from the main current.

In the Northeast, the best fishing for bonito is from late July until around Labor Day, which is when the false albacore start arriving. As the numbers of false albacore build, they tend to push out the bonito.

There is a second run of bonito in late October and, in some years, early November, after the albies leave and the waters begin to drop into the mid-50s.

Bonito are not nearly as common as false albacore in the water off the Outer Banks of North Carolina in the fall, but there is a fishable spring run. They are also found on both sides of the Atlantic, including in the Mediterranean and Black seas.

Life History

Like false albacore, very little is known about the migratory patterns and reproductive biology of bonito. They are believed to reach sexual maturity by the time they're 16 to 21 inches in length near the end of their second year, and they spawn in the western Atlantic close to shore in warm coastal waters in June and July. Again like false albacore, the bonito we catch have most likely spawned several times.

Fly Fishing

Most fly fishers agree that bonito seem to have better eyesight and tend to be more selective than false albacore. Keen eyesight makes them leader-shy, and most bonito anglers use light tippets of 8- to 12-pound test. Also, the use of fluorocarbon has become very popular in the last few years. Bonito have small mouths with large pointy, conical teeth. Fortunately for anglers, their teeth are spaced and they don't go all the way to the corner of the jaw. Since most fish are hooked in the corner of the mouth, you usually don't need a shock tippet. After landing a bonito, it's a good practice to check your tippet for nicks.

Flies should generally be small and sparse and match the local bait-fish. Because these fish grab bait with their teeth, they tend to short-strike or nip the back of the bait or fly. Flies should have very short tails, and I have learned that a long-shank hook will outperform a standard hook. Bonito have tough mouths, so sharp hooks are a necessity. Most bonito anglers use 8- or 9-weight rods. Reels should have smooth drags and hold 150 yards of 30-pound backing. For fly lines, my two top choices would be a clear intermediate and a sinking line of about 250 to 350 grains.

Hot Spots

In the Atlantic Ocean, there are two viable areas to target inshore bonito with a fly rod. The coastal waters of the Northeast provide the best opportunity for large bonito, with all of the fly-rod tippet-class and five line-class world records coming from an area I have dubbed the Bonito Triangle. The triangle runs from Long Island, New York, northeast to the islands of Martha's Vineyard and Nantucket in Massachusetts and west to the Rhode Island south-shore breachways.

Bonito arrive in these waters in late July and often stay until the first week of November. They are attracted by the numerous salt ponds and estuaries, which harbor incredible quantities of baitfish. These waters are the first to warm up along the Northeast coast. The outflows and inlets that connect the ponds to the ocean offer the shore-bound angler legitimate shots at inshore tuna. During the last few years, I have caught very few bonito in the triangle; however, the one spot that has produced well is the Bonito Bar off Nantucket Island in Massachusetts.

Every spring, the southern coast of North Carolina gets a push of bonito from Morehead City and Atlantic Beach south to the waters around Cape Fear, Wrightsville Beach, and just outside Masonboro Inlet. The fish arrive in early April and peak in mid-April to early May before heading offshore to the waters of the Gulf Stream. While these bonito are relatively small, averaging 3 to 6 pounds, they form massive schools on nearshore reefs and wrecks. You can usually spot them from a distance by the circling birds and churning whitewater as the fish crash through schools of bay anchovies and silversides.

Records

D. Gama Higgs holds the IGFA all-tackle record for Atlantic bonito at 18 pounds 4 ounces. He caught it on July 8, 1953, off Faial Island in the Canary Islands off the coast of Spain. October 2003 was quite a month for fly angler Angelo Peluso, who set three tippet-class records for bonito off Long Island, New York. On October 8, he landed an 8-pound 7-ounce bonito, breaking the 16-pound tippet record. Less than two weeks later, on October 17 he set a new 20-pound tippet mark with a 10-pound 7-ounce fish. Then on October 19 he broke his own 16-pound tippet record with a 10-pound 7-ounce fish.

As I alluded to earlier, all 13 fly-rod tippet-class (one is vacant) and five line-class world records come from the Bonito Triangle, and all are fairly recent catches. These record fish were caught from early August to early November, with most of the bigger fish taken from late October into the first few days of November. You will note that no records were recorded in September, which is usually when the more aggressive false albacore arrive in the greatest numbers in the Bonito Triangle. They tend to push the bonito out of the area. That's not to say that I haven't had days when I did well on both species in September, but usually when I take both species on the same day it's from different feeding areas.

Current IGFA Fly-Rod Records for Bonito

Tippet	Weight (lbs./oz.)	Location	Angler	Date
Male				
2	5/15	Montauk, NY	Stephen Sloan	8/12/88
4	8/6	Weekapaug, RI	John Dickinson	11/2/90
6	10/7	Fishers Island, NY	David Skok	10/27/94
8	10/9	Martha's Vineyard, MA	Kib Bramhall	10/3/89
12	12/5	Martha's Vineyard, MA	Jim Lepage	10/23/94
16	10/7	Port Jefferson Inlet, NY	Angelo Peluso	10/19/03
20	10/7	Port Jefferson Inlet, NY	Angelo Peluso	10/17/03
Female				
2	Vacant			
4	5/0	Watch Hill, RI	Gail Greenwood-Noyes	8/14/00
6	6/0	Race, NY	Gail Greenwood-Noyes	7/29/02
8	6/0	Race, NY	Gail Greenwood-Noyes	7/29/02
12	8/2	Watch Hill, RI	Gail Greenwood-Noyes	10/31/99
16	7/0	Weekapaug, RI	Gail Greenwood-Noyes	8/14/98
20	6/4	Race, NY	Gail Greenwood-Noyes	7/29/02

In addition to holding all six of the woman's tippet-class records, on October 16, 1996, Gail Greenwood-Noyes landed the 16-pound line-class world-record bonito. The 11-pound 12-ounce fish is the largest bonito ever landed in the United States by a woman. In July 2005 Gail set three fly-rod class-tippet records on bluefin tuna. The fish weighed between 18 and 21 pounds. All 10 of Gail's records were landed while fishing with her husband and guide Captain Sandy Noyes.

Skipjack (*Katsuwonus pelamis*)

Description

Skipjack tuna, also known as striped tuna and oceanic bonito, are more tapered at both ends than false albacore, giving them more of a cigar-shaped body with a sharply pointed snout. Their back is dark purplish

GENE QUIGLEY

Horizontal bars on the side and the absence of markings on the back help anglers identify skipjack.

blue, and they have silvery sides and belly. The presence of four to six dark horizontal stripes on their belly and the absence of markings on the back distinguish skipjack from other tuna species. Their mouth is relatively large, and like bonito they have small, conical teeth.

Distribution

Skipjack tuna have worldwide distribution in tropic and temperate seas and can be found in the Atlantic as far north as Massachusetts in the summer and as far south as Brazil year-round. They are common throughout the Gulf of Mexico. When feeding near the surface, skipjack can form vast schools reaching as high as fifty thousand fish. They often join in with blackfin and yellowfin tuna during a feeding frenzy.

Life History

Skipjack tuna reach sexual maturity at about 18 to 20 inches in length and two years of age. They spawn throughout the year in tropical waters and from spring to early fall in subtropical waters. While they can

Master fly tier Dave Skok admires a skipjack.

exceed 40 pounds, skipjack tend to average only 5 to 10 pounds, with fish in the teens being real trophies.

Fly Fishing

Many guides feel that skipjack are the toughest tuna, pound for pound, to tangle with on a fly rod. They are primarily an offshore fish, making only rare inshore appearances. They are usually caught by fly fishers from 1 to 10 miles off the beach, but a few have been caught from shore. Because skipjack tuna are small and unpredictable in their movements, few guides actually target them. Anglers seeking other tuna species, especially blackfin and yellowfin, often catch skipjack incidentally.

Skipjack combine the speed and power of false albacore with the erratic fight of a bonito. Offshore boat captains have nicknamed them mushmouths, due to their relatively soft mouths. When you hook into a mushy, great care should be used when applying pressure, particularly during the early stages of the battle. Eight- to 10-weight rods and reels with smooth drags and capacity for 200 yards of 30-pound backing will work nicely for skipjack.

Hot Spots

Skipjack tuna are frequently caught in the offshore canyons of the Northeast and Mid-Atlantic states, but there doesn't seem to be any pattern or predictability regarding when or if they will come inshore in any given year. In New England, when skippies do occur it is usually during the last two weeks of August and the first week of September. Newport, Rhode Island, has very deep water close to shore and frequently attracts skippies, as does Devils Bridge, which is just off the Gay Head lighthouse on Martha's Vineyard.

Records

The IGFA all-tackle record for skipjack is 45 pounds 4 ounces. Brian Evans caught this fish off Mexico's Baja on November 16, 1996. The fly-rod record is 16 pounds 1 ounce, taken by Walt Jennings off the Revillagigedo Islands of Mexico on March 20, 1996.

Current IGFA Fly-Rod Records for Skipjack Tuna

Tippet	Weight (lbs./oz.)	Location	Angler	Date
Male				
2	13/2	Piton Pointe, Mauritius	Richard F. Flasch	12/8/90
4	11/0	Le Morne, Boye, Mauritius	Richard F. Flasch	11/29/90
6	14/12	Santa Barbara, CA	Patt Wardlaw	12/7/75
8	11/6	NE Whale Island, New Zealand	Sam Mossman	2/9/96
12	15/0	Santa Barbara, CA	Patt Wardlaw	12/15/75
16	15/8	Miloii, Kona, HI	M. Schwartz	9/1/89
20	16/1	Revillagigedo Islands, Mexico	Walt Jennings	3/20/96
Female				
2	Vacant			
4	Vacant			
6	Vacant			
8	Vacant			
12	4/0	Fajardo, Puerto Rico	Wilmary Rivera	9/21/02
16	9/11	Thetis Bank, Baja, Mexico	Donna Anderson	12/4/03
20	8/5	Rockaway, NY	Joan Sharrott	8/7/99

Albacore (*Thunnus alalunga*)

Description

Albacore, also known as longfin tuna, can be distinguished from other tunas by their long pectoral fins, which can reach back past the origin of their second dorsal and anal fins. They are the only tuna that have a thin white trailing edge running along the back of the tail fin. Their back is bluish purple and their flanks are silvery gray, with no stripes or spots. They can exceed 50 pounds but usually run 20 to 40 pounds.

Albacore have beautiful, firm white meat, which gives them their nickname, "chicken of the sea." They are sought after by the canning industry and are marketed as "solid white tuna."

Distribution

Albacore are found offshore in waters measuring 40 fathoms or more, out to the deepwater canyons. They are a temperate species, found worldwide in tropical and warm temperate seas from 59 to 77 degrees Fahrenheit. They usually remain in tropical or warm waters but make occasional migrations into colder waters as far north as Nova Scotia in search of food.

MICHAEL SCHWEIT

Longfins lack the body markings common on many other tuna.

GENE QUIGLEY

A longfin albacore almost ready for the gaff

Life History

Albacore reach sexual maturity at about 36 inches in length and three years of age. They spawn in June and July in subtropical waters in both hemispheres and throughout the Mediterranean Sea.

Fly Fishing

Because albacore are usually found a great distance from shore and prefer deep water, they aren't generally targeted by fly anglers. Recently Captain Gene Quigley of *Shore Catch* has been organizing some overnight fly-fishing charters to the Hudson Canyon off New Jersey. Several of these trips produced nice catches of yellowfin tuna, with an occasional longfin albacore in the mix. Longfin albacore are commonly caught by fly-rodders who fish on the long-range boats in the Pacific Ocean off San Diego and Santa Cruz, California. In fact, four of the five tippet-class world records have come from the waters off California in the last four years.

Records

The IGFA all-tackle world record is 88 pounds 2 ounces and was taken off the Canary Islands on November 19, 1977, by Siegfried Dickemann. The fly-rod world record is 47 pounds, taken in the Hudson Canyon off New Jersey's coast on September 7, 1992, by Robert Lubarsky. This is the only IGFA fly-rod record taken out of the western Atlantic.

Bigeye (*Thunnus obesus*)

Description

Bigeye tuna are similar in general appearance to bluefin and yellowfin tuna. They have a plumper and stouter body than other tuna, a larger head, and unusually large eyes. Their long pectoral fins reach back to their second dorsal fin, and they have shorter dorsal and anal fins than yellowfin tuna do.

The best way to distinguish them from other tuna is the exceptionally large eyes in proportion to the head. Their high body fat helps to insulate them from cold water, allowing bigeye to venture into deeper waters more than their cousins do. This fat content is what makes them so attractive to the sashimi market. They usually weigh over 100 pounds and can go up to 400 pounds. Their life cycle is about five to seven years.

Distribution

Bigeye tuna can be found in the waters of the western Atlantic Ocean from southern Nova Scotia down to Brazil in South America. They are caught mainly by commercial long-liners. Because they travel far below the surface and because of their large size, they aren't targeted by fly-rodders in the western Atlantic. Adult bigeye are the deepest occurring of all tuna species, with the greatest concentrations found at depths between 150 and 250 fathoms.

Hot Spots

There is a usually a good bigeye bite south of Martha's Vineyard and Nantucket in Massachusetts in August. Off Montauk, New York, bigeyes are rarely caught inside the canyon, which is almost 70 miles from Montauk at its closest point. In New Jersey waters, a few bigeye are caught by trollers in the Hudson Canyon.

Records

The IGFA all-tackle world-record bigeye tuna weighed 392 pounds 6 ounces and was caught on July 25, 1996, by Dieter Vogel off the coast of Spain. There is only one fly-rod record of an Atlantic bigeye, a 9-pound 14-ounce fish taken on a 16-pound tippet by Christian Benazeth off Mauritania on October 23, 1991. There are several Pacific bigeye fly-rod tippet records from Japan and Hawaii, with the largest a 31-pound 8-ounce fish taken on 12-pound tippet by Tomoyoshi Kagami on June 7, 1994, off Kume Island, Japan.

Part II

Battle Plans

Gearing Up

You Don't Take a Knife to a Gunfight

It was a bluebird-calm, sunny day. Captain Corey Pietraszek and his clients were using light spinning tackle to target bass, bluefish, bonito, and false albacore just off the beach around Newport, Rhode Island. They already had one Northeast grand slam—three of the above species—for the day when a pod of schoolie bluefin tuna erupted 75 feet off the bow. Before Corey realized it, one of his clients had tossed a Hopkins lure into the school and was tight to a 100-pound-plus tuna.

His reel screamed, whined, and sputtered as the fish melted off 200 yards of 14-pound test line, spooling the reel in less than 20 seconds. The angler just stood there staring at his tackle in shock and disbelief as he asked Corey, "What the hell just happened?" Corey replied simply, "You don't take a knife to a gunfight."

Being undergunned is a common problem for anglers running into tuna. On another outing, Corey reports that his clients were fishing for bonito using 8- and 9-weight fly rods. They decided to take advantage of a midday lull and have a lunch break. The angler fishing from the bow left his line ready on the deck in case fish showed up. (I can't begin to tell you how many times I've been halfway through a sandwich when all hell breaks loose around the boat, with tuna crashing bait on the surface. For me, this usually means a dumped sandwich and a cold beverage spilling all over my tackle.)

Sure enough, just as the anglers started to eat their lunch, a pod of fish busted on bait less than 60 feet off the bow. One jumped up, grabbed his fly rod, and made a perfect cast into the fray. Two strips on the line, and he was hooked up to what he instantly found out was a bluefin tuna that Corey estimated at about 75 pounds. In his excitement, the angler put too much pressure on the fish, and his rod snapped about 2 feet up from the reel seat. He continued the fight with the rod he had left, but in a matter of seconds, his 8-weight reel got spooled and the line snapped. He lost the front 7 feet of his rod, his entire fly line, and all his backing.

As Corey tells the story, the frustrated angler then ran back to the boat's center console, grabbed the remaining half of his roast beef sandwich, and threw it in the direction of the fish, hollering, "Keep the change, you filthy animal!"

Prior to targeting tuna with a fly rod, I thought I'd seen every possible way to lose a fish: hooks straightening, knots failing, rods breaking. With tuna, I've added several new methods to this repertoire, including broken fly lines and anglers with broken bodies and spirits. I have seen huge guys who looked like they worked out daily get so exhausted that they had to just give up and hand their rods over to another angler. Several charter captains have told me stories of a single large tuna exhausting their entire six-man charter party as they took turns on the rod. Tuna are tough fish, and you better be at the top of your game if you decide to target them.

Speak Softly and Carry a Big Stick

If you're going to fly fish for tuna, keep in mind the old adage, "Speak softly and carry a big stick." The smaller tuna, including bonito, skipjack, false albacore, and most blackfin, can be taken comfortably on 10-weight rods. But when you start targeting their larger cousins, yellowfin and bluefin, you'll want at least a 12-weight, and in most cases you would be better served with a 13- or 14-weight rod. As a general rule, if you're chasing tuna in the 10- to 25-pound range, a 10- or 11-weight rod is fine. For fish from 25 to 50 pounds, I'd recommend a 12- or 13-weight, and for fish from 50 to 100 pounds, a 14-weight is strongly recommended.

If you plan to target tuna over 100 pounds on a fly, first I recommend you see a shrink, then increase your life insurance and get the name of a good chiropractor. If you're still game, use at least a 14-weight rod and consider going up to a 16- to 19-weight stick—and may the gods be with you! There are only a handful of anglers who have taken a 100-pound bluefin tuna with a fly rod, and no one has yet landed a 100-pound yellowfin on a fly.

If you aren't certain what size fish you're likely to encounter, I suggest using a 14-weight rod. It is light enough to cast a fly, is strong enough to quickly land a 30-pound fish for release, and has the guts to lift a 100-pound fish. The key to landing larger tuna is lifting power. You need to be able to get the fish's head up or it will take you to the cleaners. During the final stages of battle, tuna will sulk deep directly below the boat, and your struggle becomes vertical. It is during this lifting stage that the tuna tests the limits of the rod and the will and stamina of the angler.

Ten years ago you would have been hard pressed to find a rod manufacturer that made a 14-weight rod. In the late 1980s, the largest rod you could find was a 12-weight, which was used for tarpon. In 1991, the Fisher Rod Company came out with a 15-weight rod. Today there are dozens of companies making 14-weight rods, with several producing 15- to 17-weights, and Cape Fear even manufactures a 19-weight rod.

Tuna rods have to serve the dual purposes of casting and lifting. For casting, the rod has to bend under the load of the line, and to lift a fish's head the rod needs to have stiffness. Most tuna-rod manufacturers try to accommodate both goals by having the top third of the rod bend under the load of the fly line for casting and the lower two-thirds considerably stiffer than traditional rods to provide the necessary lifting power.

JOE LECLAIR

When the fight goes vertical, a stiff fly rod can make all the difference.

Anglers usually have to make a compromise. Generally, a good casting rod isn't a good lifting rod, and vice versa. My preference is a rod with good lifting strength. In bluewater fishing, you aren't going to make a lot of casts, and normally you won't need a long cast. If fish are breaking on top, your boat will get you into casting range. When fish aren't visible, you can troll until you locate them and chum or chunk them into range.

Lifting a strong fish's head vertically is the most physically demanding aspect of fly fishing. (You lift the head in order to gain line.) Lift the rod up and then wind in line as you lower the rod. To prevent breaking rods, especially graphite, the vertical lift should start well below a horizontal position and stop just above it. This puts the load on the butt of the rod, which is the strongest section. If your rod doesn't have the guts to lift the fish, you'll burn out your back and arm muscles before you're able to land it.

Things to Look for in a Tuna Stick

You need a fighting butt that you can press against your body or a fighting belt to gain leverage on the fish. This is particularly important in the final stages of the fight, as you're lifting the fish. A fighting butt is a 2- to 3-inch extension at the butt of the rod. It serves as a pivot point when

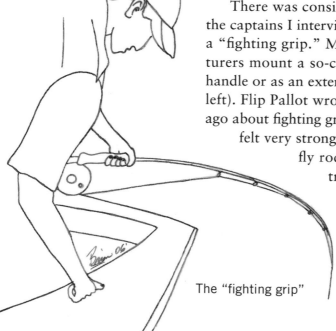

The "fighting grip"

pumping the fish and also keeps the reel away from your body when you're reeling in line.

There was considerable disagreement among the captains I interviewed as to the importance of a "fighting grip." Most bluewater rod manufacturers mount a so-called fighting grip above the handle or as an extension of the handle (shown at left). Flip Pallot wrote an article almost a decade ago about fighting grips in which he stated that he felt very strongly that they have no place on fly rods and that they actually detract from the angler's ability to fight the fish.

He argued that when you slide your hand up to the grip, the section below your hand gets taken out of the equation, and

that is the most powerful part of the rod. Holding the rod at the fighting grip moves the pressure of the fight toward the tip.

Pallot went on to explain that in fighting large fish, leverage is the key. By keeping the angle of your rod low, the pressure is put on the butt section of the rod, which is the section designed to fight fish (see illustration on opposite page).

Conversely, if your rod tip is held high, the pressure is on the tip section, which is the section designed for casting (see illustration above). You simply can't land large fish by fighting them with the rod tip. The only time I use the fighting grip is when the fish makes its first few long runs. I point the rod almost directly at the fish and let the reel's drag do all the work. By moving my hand up to the fighting grip, I form a triangle with my back and arms straight and relaxed, in effect resting them for the battle ahead.

For me the fighting grip is a resting grip, although I hesitate to use the word "resting" when talking about fighting tuna. As any tuna captain will tell you, the only time to rest when you're hooked to a tuna is when it lands on the boat's deck. Most novice anglers get so pumped up when they hook a tuna that even when the fish is taking line they're pulling back on the rod, unnecessarily straining their arms instead of letting the reel's drag tire the fish.

JOE LECLAIR

Tuna demand first-rate equipment.

Most fly rods are made of graphite, but more and more of the blue-water rod manufacturers are using a graphite-fiberglass composite. When used in conjunction with graphite, fiberglass increases the rod's durability, making it a more efficient lifting machine. Also, with the tougher composites, if you do choke up on the rod by using the fighting grip you can still apply sufficient pressure without breaking the rod. This is more comfortable for the angler. The downside is that it moves the load farther up the rod, and this could cause a graphite blank to shatter.

Reel seats are extremely important on bluewater rods—always take your reel with you when you're trying out a new rod to make certain you get a good, tight fit. You'll also want double-locking nuts to ensure that the reel doesn't come loose during the battle.

One captain relayed a story of an angler whose reel came off during a fight with a tuna and ripped its way up the rod, tearing through all the guides and hesitating only briefly at the tip before taking the entire tip section of the two-piece outfit down to Davey Jones' locker. The puzzled angler was left holding just the butt section of his rod—no tip section, no line, no reel.

Today's multipiece rods are so well made and durable that I strongly recommend you purchase three- or four-piece rods, especially for travel.

I have learned through experience that a traveling fisherman should never be separated from his fishing gear. Clothes and personal items are easy to replace, but trying to replace lost fishing equipment can be difficult and expensive and could even ruin an otherwise great fishing trip. (However, I have found in my travels since 9/11 that airport security frequently doesn't even allow fishing reels with line to be carried onboard.)

Another thing I like about multipiece rods is that they are easy to store on boats, enabling me to carry several backup outfits. Backups aren't a luxury on a tuna trip. They are an absolute necessity, as evidenced by the next story.

Sarge Goes Overboard

I was initially reluctant to include this story for fear it would embarrass one of the best charter captains I've ever fished with. Out of respect for his knowledge, skill, and work ethic, I will refer to him as "Sarge," a nickname my annual Florida albie fest crew gave him because of the way he barks out orders during sieges. Believe me, when Sarge gives orders, his clients follow them. On a recent trip, my fishing partner Peter McCarthy and I were doubled up on two good-sized albies; we were near the end of the battles when the fish crisscrossed our lines. Sarge barked, "What the hell are you two dumb 'bleepity bleeps' doing, making macramé?"

In an effort to undo the mess we'd created, Sarge grabbed both rods and starting unwinding our "macramé." Suddenly Peter's fish surged and his rod slipped out of Sarge's wet hand. In a split second the quick-thinking captain, in one fluid motion, tossed me my rod and dove head-first overboard after Peter's outfit. As Sarge cleared the rail, his foot inadvertently kicked my outfit out of my hand and into the drink.

Sarge wasn't the only one holding his breath for the next few moments, but alas, only the drenched, red-faced captain made it back into the boat. Everyone felt bad, not only for the loss of our equipment but also for Sarge, because we knew he felt terrible. Finally, Peter broke the icy silence by saying, "Let's fish until we run out of tackle!" It was early in the day, and the fishing had been fabulous. Although we were sorely disappointed about losing our gear, our trip wasn't ruined because we had backup equipment.

That day still stands as the hardest on tackle I've ever experienced. We had a total of six anglers fishing from two boats, and the death toll for the day was two complete outfits lost overboard, three rods broken, and two fly lines destroyed. This is a record I hope never to approach

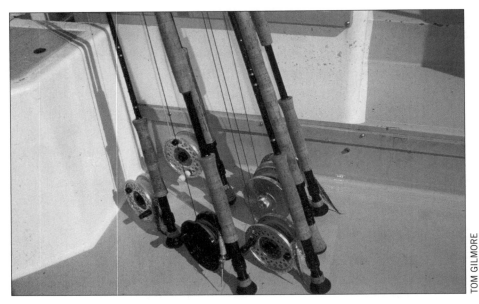

You can never have enough fishing outfits on a bluewater trip.

again. After the trip, Sarge tried to pay us for the lost equipment. When we wouldn't take his money, he said the three days of fishing were on him. When that was unacceptable, we compromised; our next trip will be on Sarge.

Reels

Fly reels can be very expensive, but when you're tight to the tuna of a lifetime you'll thank God for your wise investment. A reel should have enough line capacity to hold a fly line and at least 400 yards of backing. Tuna rarely run off more than 200 yards, and if they do you can follow them. The typical tuna battle usually consists of a few long blistering runs followed by swift descents to the depths below, with the tuna pushing down as far as it can take you. When tuna go down, you need to have the backing capacity to stop them.

Tuna are faster than most fish, and they don't waste energy jumping —they just bear down at speeds in excess of 40 mph and try to smoke you. You and your reel's drag will be screaming for mercy. In addition to line capacity and a reel with a smooth, tough drag, you should consider the advantage a large-arbor reel has to offer.

Today's large-arbor reels have a larger arbor and a larger-diameter spool. This enables you to retrieve more line per revolution than with traditional arbors, thereby increasing the speed of line retrieval. After a tuna takes a fly and makes its initial run, it will often turn and come back toward the pressure, throwing slack in the line. A large-arbor reel will help you take up the slack more efficiently and keep constant pressure on the fish.

Some reels have a very small drag-adjustment nut that needs to move only a short distance to change the drag setting from light to maximum. These reels can be a disaster when you're fighting big tuna, because it's too easy to overadjust the drag setting during the battle, which usually results in a broken tippet. You want a drag adjustment that changes over a wide range.

Many anglers will tell you to never touch your drag when fighting a fish, and that's certainly good advice, especially if your reel has the small drag-adjustment range. Instead of adjusting the drag, you can put additional pressure on the fish by palming the reel. But if you're going to palm your spool when fighting larger tuna, I strongly recommend that you wear a glove to protect your hand.

I like to set my drag light. If I need additional pressure during the initial runs I'll palm the reel, but once the fish goes deep and I have to start lifting, I'll tighten up my drag setting. I pinch the line against the rod's cork handle as I lift, but if the fish starts to run I'll let go and let

A selection of bluewater rods and reels

GENE QUIGLEY

the drag stop it. I find I can land the fish more quickly with the additional pressure from the drag.

You have a choice between direct-drag or anti-reverse reels; I prefer the traditional direct-drive models. The handle is attached directly to the spool, and basically the spool does what you and the handle tell it to do. Direct-drive reels are easier to clean and maintain, and I like having the option of increasing the pressure I put on a fish by palming the exposed spool. I also want a reel with a large handle to reduce the likelihood of my fingers cramping during a prolonged fight. The only downside I see to direct-drive reels is that a speeding tuna will make your reel spin at blinding speed, and it's not uncommon to have your knuckles whacked by the handle.

When a fish takes line from an anti-reverse reel, the handle remains in position. Recently, some manufacturers have begun offering anti-reverse reels with exposed spools. This allows the angler to palm the spool, a nice feature not available on earlier models. Certain professionals such as doctors and dentists, whose patients might not appreciate battle-scarred hands, should consider anti-reverse reels.

Lines

The early pioneers of bluewater fly fishing didn't have access to the vast array of specialty lines we have today, so many developed their own shooting-head systems. Shooting heads had many advantages over the existing fly lines. They enable the angler to quickly "shoot" a fly to the fish, as you can load the rod with only one back cast. And they are easy to change, allowing the angler to fish with different-weight lines depending on where the fish are in the water column.

Another advantage of a shooting-head system is that it leaves more space on the reel for backing, and the shorter head produces very little drag in the water because the running line is much thinner than on standard fly lines. This is very important when fishing lighter-class tippets, which could break under the pressure of a full fly line dragging through the water.

As I mentioned earlier, I don't normally chase records, so when targeting the larger tuna species I use tippets in excess of 20 pounds. With these stronger tippets, fly-line drag is much less of a problem. Recently, anglers choosing to push the envelope with bigger rods and stronger tippets found the weak link to be the fly line itself. Most traditional fly lines have a core strength of about 35 pounds. As bluewater fly fishing became more popular, line manufacturers began developing specialty lines. Over time, these lines incorporated stronger cores, a continuous knotless transition from running line to shooting head, and greater overall length.

I like a longer line because I'm more confident pushing my tackle and Mr. Tuna to the limit when I have my fly line on the reel. The fly line I use is stronger than my backing, and once it's on the reel, two knots are taken out of the battle. One of the main reasons for shorter fly lines was that they allowed more room for backing. This need has been offset by large-arbor reels, which have more capacity. Also, with the new stronger and thinner backing materials, you can literally put close to a half mile of backing on some reels.

I use a golf glove on my rod hand when fighting tuna, so I can use my index finger to guide the backing smoothly across the reel's spool. The glove protects my hand from line cuts, which can be nasty, especially from the gel-spun backing materials that have become so popular in big-game fishing.

Currently, I fish fly lines manufactured by Rio Products. A few years back Rio, working with First Light Anglers from Rowley, Massachusetts, developed a fly line for targeting the school-sized bluefin tuna that were becoming popular targets off Cape Cod. I had a few lines from the initial run and loved them. These prototype lines proved so popular that in 2005 Rio marketed them as part of their Leviathan series. They come with both sinking and intermediate heads.

Today most reputable manufacturers produce a bluewater series of fly lines. When possible, I like to fish a clear or translucent intermediate line with a short weight-forward head. These lines don't spook fish, and intermediates are easier to pick up and recast than sinking lines. I really believe clear lines and fluorocarbon leaders give you an edge, especially when drifting a fly back into a chum slick.

Leaders and Tippet

Monofilament versus fluorocarbon. Let's set the record straight right from the beginning. For many species of fish, I question the need to spend the extra money on fluorocarbon. For tuna, however, I believe fluorocarbon is a must. The refractive index of fluorocarbon is almost identical to the water's, making it nearly invisible. It is denser and sinks faster than monofilament, and it's more resistant to abrasion. One word of caution: Because fluorocarbon is harder and slicker than mono, it often needs an extra twist or turn in knots to make it hold correctly.

Tuna have keen eyesight and small teeth that can wear through tippet, so play it safe and stick with fluorocarbon. Too often we anglers invest most of our money on the wrong end of the battle line. As Lefty Kreh likes to say, "Fishing is a jerk on one end of a line waiting for a jerk on the other end." My recommendation is to spend your money on the fish's end first.

How often have you heard anglers complain when they have to spend $10 for tippet material or $15 for a dozen hooks? And they are outraged when a custom fly tier using the finest hooks and materials gets $9 or $10 for a fly. Yet these same anglers have no problem spending thousands of dollars on their fishing vehicles, boats, guides' fees, rods, reels, and lines. If you don't invest your money on the fish's end of your line—hooks, flies, tippet—the rest of your money will be wasted.

That being said, several of the Gulf of Mexico tuna guides I interviewed feel that fluorocarbon is a gimmick that's not worth the extra money. These same guides are so spoiled by their great fishery that they complain about having to "cull" through blackfin, which they often use for chum, to get to yellowfin. If I had that problem in the Northeast where I usually fish, I wouldn't be so anal about my leaders, tackle, and knots either.

Most of the tuna experts I interviewed don't fish for records. They feel that by not having to fish IGFA leaders they can keep things simple, with fewer knots. And by using heavier leaders they have more options for knot selection. The nice thing about going to a heavier leader is that you don't need a bite tippet, which allows you to eliminate at least one knot in your leader system.

The downside of going heavier is that most 13- and 14-weight rods can deadlift only about 20 pounds without breaking. If you're using a fly line with a 70-pound core and a leader of 40 pounds with a 12- to 14-weight rod, you may shatter your rod if you're not careful. Rod manufacturers are seeing more and more broken rods, and one manufacturer's rep told me that many companies are considering limiting the warranties on their heavier rods. Most guides use a very simple leader, often just a straight shot of about 4 to 6 feet of 30- to 40-pound fluorocarbon.

I used this same system until I encountered one incredible all-night tuna blitz in the Gulf of Mexico. That night our party of four put about 80 tuna in the boat, most of them blackfin up to 20 pounds, but we did

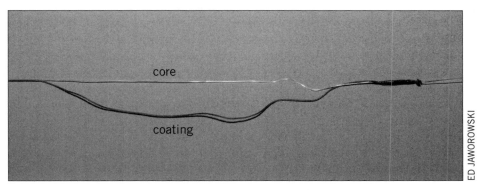

core

coating

ED JAWOROWSKI

Broken line

land four yellowfin up to 65 pounds. We also lost several larger yellowfin, and between the fish we landed and lost, our tackle took quite a beating.

I discovered two problems with the straight length of 25-pound fluorocarbon we were using. One was that the relatively thin tippet material cut through the fly line coating; fortunately, the fly lines we were using had 60-pound test cores and didn't break. The second problem did cost us a few fish and damaged our fly lines to the point that we had to replace them. The larger yellowfin were actually longer than our leaders, which enabled the tuna to batter the loop-to-loop connection between fly line and leader with their tails.

A tuna's tail is hard and strong and cycles at speeds of up to 30 times per second. It can wear through a knot, even a fly line, and on that trip we had tuna shatter both leader and fly-line knots. The 65-pound yellowfin I landed had done so much damage to the first 18 inches of my fly line that the core and the coating were torn apart. I was able to repair the line later but had to change spools in order to continue fishing. Now when I fish for large tuna, I use a heavy 5-foot butt section and attach 3 feet of tippet using a surgeon's knot.

Knots

When you think about it, being able to tie good knots has to be the most important skill of a tuna fisherman. If you can't tie perfect knots at or near 100 percent of the line strength, you're doomed to fail. In addition to being strong, the knots must be able to pass over your rod guides without snagging. On many occasions I've seen knots jam into a fly-rod guide and break off the fish, the guide, and even the rod itself. That's why I love loops. Interlocking loops, when done correctly, are strong and can sail through the guides with ease. Loops also allow you to change fly line, leaders, and tippets easily.

Backing Knots

The knot I choose for the loop in my backing depends on the type of backing I use. My reels for bonito, false albacore, skipjack, and blackfin tuna are filled with 30-pound Dacron backing. Dacron is hollow, which enables you to splice the tag end back through itself, forming a knotless loop. This is referred to as a "no knot" backing splice, or a blind splice. You will need a piece of thin, single-strand, stainless steel wire to make this splice. I recommend a 20-inch piece of No. 2 or 3 trolling wire.

Blind Splice

1. Fold the wire in half and pinch the fold to a point.

Bend wire

2. Insert the wire about 2 feet above the tag end of the backing. For ease of changing lines, you'll want the loop to be large enough to slip over a reel or fly-line spool.
3. Insert the point end of the wire into the hollow core of the Dacron and work the wire for 4 to 6 inches toward the tag end of the backing. Once you have the wire inside the Dacron the desired distance, push it outside the braid.

Insert wire

4. Insert the tag end of the Dacron into the loop on the wire and pull it out the other side about an inch.

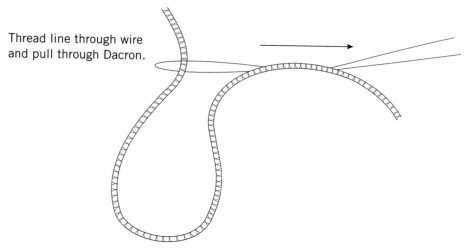

Thread line through wire and pull through Dacron.

5. Hold the two tag ends of the wire and pull the tag end of the Dacron back inside and through the core of the Dacron. Continue pulling until the wire and line tag exit the core. Now you can adjust the size of the loop by gently pulling on the tag to shorten the loop or on the loop end to increase it.

6. You can now tighten the loop by pulling on it with one hand while pulling on the standing line with the other. This forces the hollow core to squeeze down and tighten, like a Chinese finger puzzle. While this is a very dependable knot, I like to add a second splice about an inch above the first by repeating steps two through five.

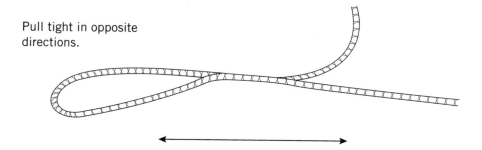

Pull tight in opposite directions.

7. Trim the tag end of the second splice so that it ends inside the core of the second splice.

8. Apply a small amount of flexible glue for about 1/2 inch at the tag end of the rear splice.

On my bluefin and yellowfin reels I use gel-spun backing. This backing is extremely thin, so you can greatly increase the amount of backing you put on your reel and the pound test. I generally use 65-pound test, as it is a little thicker than 50-pound and packs better on the spool. Unlike Dacron, gel-spun backings aren't hollow, so you can't form a loop using the blind splice. The following are two options; one is a simple surgeon's loop, the other a Bimini twist.

Surgeon's Loop

The surgeon's loop is a quick, simple, and serviceable loop knot. It can be tied in a matter of seconds and has a 95 percent breaking strength, which is more than adequate with a gel-spun backing of at least 50-pound test.

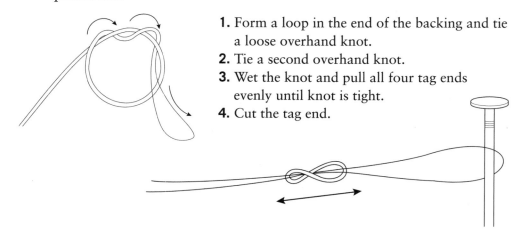

1. Form a loop in the end of the backing and tie a loose overhand knot.
2. Tie a second overhand knot.
3. Wet the knot and pull all four tag ends evenly until knot is tight.
4. Cut the tag end.

Bimini Twist

This is an almost legendary knot. It is probably the most frequently used knot in offshore and tropical flats fly fishing. It is also the most discussed knot, with anglers debating how many turns it requires and how to complete it. Certainly any angler with a reputation for tying a good Bimini has extra cachet in the angling community. When tied correctly, the Bimini twist is a 100 percent–strength loop knot. This is a very popular knot to use when fishing IGFA tippet-class leaders.

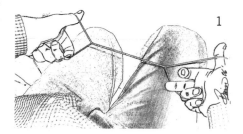

1

1. Double the end of your line to form a large loop. Placing the end of the loop over one hand and

holding the two strands of line in the other, make 20 turns or twists in the line by rotating your hand.

2. Place the loop over something firm (many anglers use their knee or foot) and pull on both the tag and line ends of the line, forcing the twists together.

3. Hook the index finger of one hand inside the loop and slide it upward to tighten the twists. Make certain you have tension on all the strands of line during this step. As the twists are tightening, hold the tag end of the line at a right angle to the standing line and allow the line to roll down over the twists. The outer wraps need to be very close together and completely cover the twists.

4. With the wraps held tightly in place by your index finger still inside the loop, make a half hitch around one leg of the loop with the tag end and then pull it up tight to secure the wraps of the Bimini. You can now ease up on the line tension without the wraps unraveling.

5. Form a semicircle with the tag end and make four or five turns over both "legs" of the Bimini loop, passing the tag through the semicircle with each wrap, working back toward the bottom of the column of the barrel wraps. Moisten the knot and pull the tag ends slowly, forcing the spirals to bunch up tightly.

6. Snug everything down and trim the tag end.

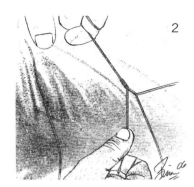

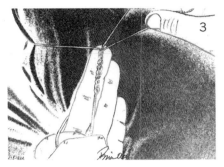

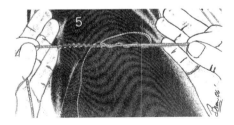

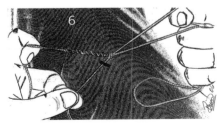

No matter what loop you use on gel-spun backing, when you connect it to the fly line it's a good idea to take the backing loop over the fly-line loop two or three times. These extra wraps minimize the chance of the backing cutting through the fly line.

Fly-Line Loops

For years I have used a simple whipped loop at both ends of my fly line. Properly tied, this knot should never break or catch on the guides. And these loops allow you to easily change fly lines and leaders using loop-to-loop connections.

1. Taper the tip of the fly line by cutting it on a 45-degree angle with a safety razor blade.
2. Fold the fly line back about ¾ inch.
3. Take a fly-tying bobbin and wrap the thread around one leg of the bobbin about three times to increase tension. Make several wraps around the two sides of the fly line.
4. Next, swing the bobbin around the loop. The faster the swing, the more the thread will bite into the fly line and secure the loop. Wrap until you have only about ¼ inch of loop left in the fly line.
5. To finish the knot, form a loop in a short piece of 8-pound mono. Lay this against the whipped loop and make eight or nine wraps with the bobbin over the mono and against the whipped section of the loop.
6. Cut the tying thread and slip it through the mono loop. Pull both tag ends of the mono, thus pulling the end of the thread under the wraps.
7. Coat with a flexible cement like Pliobond.

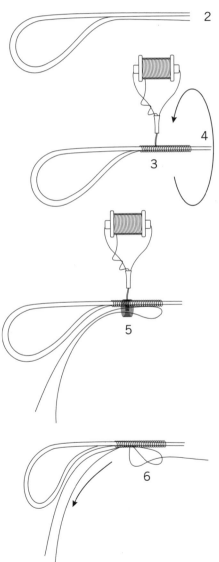

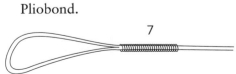

Leader and Tippet Knots

When not fishing IGFA-class leaders and tippets, I like to keep my knots simple. That way I can tie them with confidence under even the most difficult of circumstances. The following knots have served me well and can be tied in the face of wind, rain, low light, and even blitzing tuna.

Interlocking Loop-to-Loop Connection

For the loop on the butt end of my leader, I use a simple surgeon's loop. To connect the butt of the leader to the fly line, I use an interlocking loop-to-loop connection.

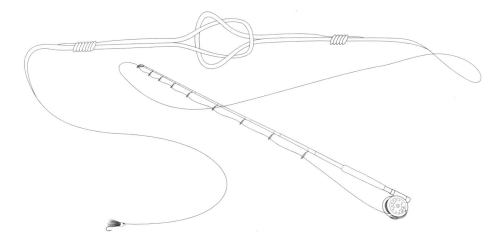

Surgeon's Knot

A surgeon's knot is similar to the surgeon's loop. It's very simple and when tied properly it doesn't slip, even when joining leaders of different diameters or strengths. It has a 95 percent breaking strength, and it's my first choice for tying the tippet section to the leader.

1. Place the leader and tippet parallel and overlap for about 12 inches.

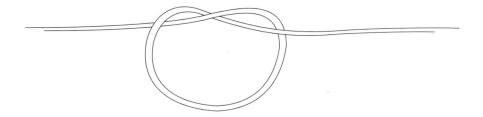

2. Tie an overhand knot, pulling the entire tippet through the loop.

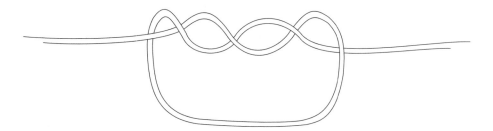

3. Tie a second overhand knot.

4. Wet the knot and pull all four tag ends evenly until the knot is tight.
5. Trim the tag ends.

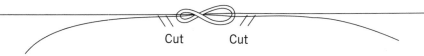

Cut   Cut

Nonslip Mono Loop

The nonslip mono loop is my go-to knot for attaching my fly. While it is a little more difficult than some other knots, I feel it is more than worth the time to master. It has 100 percent breaking strength and lets even small flies "swim" freely, no matter how heavy the tippet.

1. Tie a loose overhand knot about 6 to 8 inches from the tag end of the tippet.
2. Run the end of the tippet through the hook eye and back through the overhand knot.
3. Wrap the tag end around the standing line three or four times and take it back through the overhand knot as if you were tying a clinch knot.
4. Wet knot and uniformly tighten.

IGFA Class-Tippet Leader

Since I rarely fish for records, when I decided that I needed to put an IGFA class-tippet leader system in this book, I turned to Northeast guide Sandy Noyes for help. Sandy has guided his wife, Gail, to more fly-rod tippet-class world records for tuna than any other angler on the planet. Gail currently holds all six women's tippet-class records for bonito and all three tippet-class records for bluefin tuna.

To meet IGFA standards, the class tippet must be at least 15 inches from knot to knot. If you're adding a shock tippet, it can't exceed 12 inches, including the knot. Sandy's leader systems incorporate Bimini twists on both ends of the class tippet. He joins the tippet to the butt section with a loop-to-loop connection. Because the butt is usually 30-pound test or more, a surgeon's loop is fine on this section. To connect the class tippet to the shock tippet, Sandy uses an Albright knot (see below).

Now let's put together a sample IGFA class-tippet leader. To join the butt of the leader to the fly line, use an interlocking loop-to-loop connection. Connect the fly line's whipped loop to the butt section of the leader with a Bimini loop. The class tippet has Bimini loops at both ends. Tie a surgeon's loop in one of the Bimini twists and connect to the butt by interlocking the two loops. (This gives you a double loop in the butt section.) Take the other end of the Bimini and tie it to the shock tippet using an Albright knot. Tie the shock tippet to the fly using a nonslip mono loop.

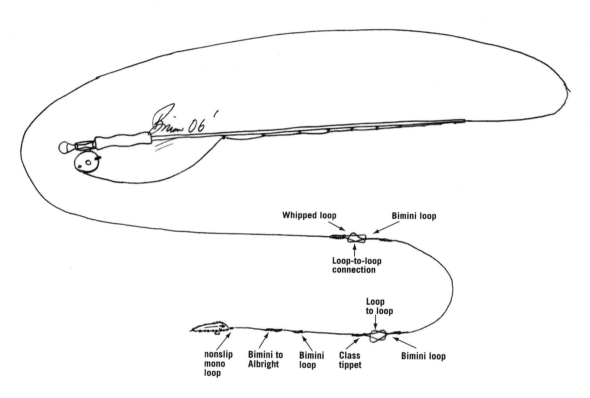

Sample IGFA class-tippet leader

Albright Knot

The Albright knot is one of the most reliable for joining lines of greatly unequal diameters.

1. Form a loop in the shock tippet material and push the tag end of the class tippet's Bimini loop through this loop.
2. Take the tag end of the Bimini and make eight to ten wraps around all three strands, working from left to right.

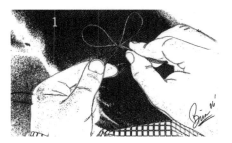 

3. After the last wrap, insert the Bimini's tag end out through the shock tippet's loop.
4. Slowly tighten by alternately pulling on the tag end of the Bimini and the standing end of the shock tippet.

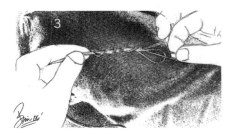 

The combination of the Albright and Bimini knots, when tied properly, gives you 100 percent strength of the class tippet. If you do fish with Bimini loop connections on your leader, tie them in advance of your trip and tie several spares. When you need to change a tippet on the water it's usually after an encounter with a fish. And when there are fish around I don't want to waste time tying knots. I also don't tie a good Bimini with nervously shaking hands, especially in a rocking boat.

Teddy Patlen, a great fly tier and "knot nut," showed me a neat trick he learned from Lefty Kreh for storing pretied class-tippet sections. He takes a full spool of tippet material, pulls the entire line off the spool, and cuts it into desired lengths. He then ties Biminis on both ends of the tippet sections and wraps them back onto the spool, using loop-to-loop connections between each section. When he needs a class-tippet section, he just unlocks the loops and is ready to go.

Specialty Tackle

Fighting Belts

A fighting belt holds the butt section of the rod in place, helps you put additional leverage on the fish, and avoid bumps and bruises on your midsection. For fly fishing, you want a belt with a closed oval cup, not one with an open top, as your rod is usually held in a nearly horizontal position when the fish is taking line. Pressure from the fish would pop the butt of the rod out of the open cup.

First Light Anglers recommends a belt manufactured by Anglers' Choice; it has an oval cup with a removable stainless-steel gimbal pin and a Velcro-nylon belt that makes it easy to switch anglers. This belt is a bargain at $19.95 and comes with a lifetime warranty.

Binoculars

Studying the seabirds in your area is a great way to spend some time when the fish aren't showing. And observing bird behavior can increase your fishing success and help you read the water. I suggest you purchase a good set of binoculars and a basic field guide for bird identification.

Binoculars for the beach or boat should have some specific attributes. They should obviously have a waterproof guarantee—not "water resistant" or "splash proof" or any other variation. True waterproof binoculars can actually be submerged (to modest depths) and are easily cleaned by immersion in fresh water. This is especially important around salt water. The only safe way to remove the salt that inevitably dries on your optics is with clean freshwater.

Binoculars for use on boats should be well armored and able to withstand the occasional bounce on the deck. Consider the warranty on your optics as well. Many of the finer binoculars feature lifetime warranties against almost anything. This will pay for itself very quickly if something goes wrong.

Power, or magnification, is perhaps the most overrated part of the binocular equation. Seven or eight times magnification (the first number on the binoculars specifications; e.g., 8x42) and an objective lens of at least 40 millimeters (the second number) should provide more than enough brightness and a large enough field of view for most fishing situations.

I recommend staying away from the higher-powered binoculars, especially if you plan to use them on a boat. Remember, you are magnifying everything, including the movement of the boat. Higher-powered binoculars are difficult to hold still when the boat is constantly pitching.

A nice yellowfin tuna taken on Jeff Pierce's flying fish fly

Rich Murphy's Pamet River Special; Rabbit Strip Baitfish from First Light Anglers; and Dave Skok's Mushmouth (left to right)

Bob Popovics' Shady Lady Squid; Capt. Gene Quigley's Tuna Squid; and Quigley's
Scallop Gut (left to right)

Clouser Minnow (left); Popovics' Jiggy (middle top); Popovics' Deep Candy (middle bottom); Quigley's Marabou Head Chunk (right top); and Quigley's Butter Chunk (right bottom)

Lefty's Deceiver (left); Blane Chocklett's Squid (middle); Chocklett's Gummy Minnow (right top); and Scott Hamilton's Hamilton Special (right bottom)

Dave Skok's Mushy Squid (left top); Jeff Pierce's Rabbit Strip (left bottom); Pierce's Ballyhoo (middle left); Skok's Mega Mushy (middle right); Pierce's Flying Fish (right)

A large yellowfin's death spiral

TOM GILMORE

Unlike most fish, tuna are warm-blooded.

TOM GILMORE

A dragger working near the Mud Hole off the Rhode Island coast

Fighting Techniques

Getting Ready to Tackle Tuna

Okay, let's assume your gear and tackle are in top shape. What about you? Are you mentally and physically prepared to tackle tuna? A lot of anglers want that hero shot with a big fish, but tuna are stronger, faster, and tougher than most fish. They don't waste energy with aerial displays like tarpon and billfish do. And after a few long, blistering runs, they usually sound deep so you can't follow them with the boat. When they do sound, the battle becomes long and vertical, and a vertical battle is the toughest for an angler and his gear to survive. Depending on the outcome of the contest, you will be physically and emotionally rewarded or completely drained.

One of my fishing partners, who has landed several 50-plus-pound sailfish in less than 20 minutes each, was so exhausted during his first fight with a bluefin tuna that he had to give up and hand over his rod 35 minutes into the fight. He hadn't seen the fish, but based on his previous experiences with sailfish he was certain it was well over 100 pounds. You should have seen the expression of disbelief on his face when his fellow angler landed the 55-pound bluefin 10 minutes after taking over the rod.

After battling my first large fly-rod tuna, I changed my whole approach to targeting these creatures. Before that trip, I thought I had really done my homework. I had the finest tackle money could buy and good knots and rigging, but I lacked experience in tuna-fighting techniques. Poor decisions and technique during the 75-minute fight exhausted me, despite the fact that I was in pretty good shape. I lost the fish

JOE LECLAIR

Make sure you're in good shape before tangling with tuna. Note the fighting belt.

boatside. My arms ached so much that I could barely cut the steak I had for dinner that night. And my back was so sore that I struggled to get in and out of my car for several days. I learned the hard way that you need to be physically *and* mentally prepared for a long, tough battle.

You really have to have the will to win or a large tuna will whip your butt. During a sustained fight your back and arms will feel like they're on fire, and the temptation to hand off the rod will be incredible. Now when I hook a good tuna, I always tell the crew, "No matter what I say later on, the only time someone else can touch this rod is after I land the fish or die!" Usually an angler's forearms give out first, so I suggest doing bicep and wrist curls with weights for several months before your trip to get your arms in tuna shape.

Run and Gun versus Stealth

Tuna blitzing on the surface of the water will turn mild-mannered, patient fly fishers into run-and-gun-crazed fiends, which often leads to what I call boat rage. Tuna can get anglers so excited that they forget on-the-water etiquette and race their boats past others, running right at and often through a school of fish, which usually puts the fish down or splits up the school. Thoughtless boaters can break through acres of churning tuna, leaving the area with only a handful of small pods of fish and ruining the fishing for everyone.

There is quite a difference of opinion as to whether motors actually spook tuna. I have caught several species of tuna in the prop wash, just a dozen feet behind the motor. I have also caught plenty of fish with the motor at idle. Some days when we're stemming the tide, the motor doesn't seem to bother tuna at all; on other days it puts them down. On occasion, just the noise from the waves slapping against the boat has been enough to put tuna on the run. But a run-and-gun approach with a racing motor will almost always put them down.

I think the best way to approach blitzing fish with a boat is to get up-current and drift down toward the fish. This way the tuna will be feeding toward you and facing into the current, and you can present your fly to the bigger, more aggressive fish at the head of the school.

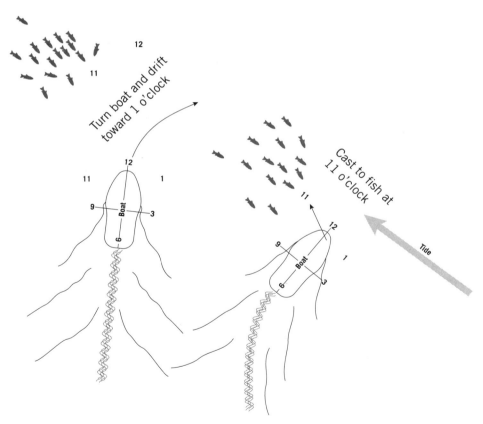

Approaching fish from a moving boat

One of the biggest challenges in fishing from a moving boat is staying in contact with your fly. If you motor cautiously toward a feeding school, the boat will continue to drift after you cut the engine. If your cast is straight forward at 12 o'clock you most likely won't be able to strip fast enough to remove the slack caused by the drifting boat. A better idea is to turn the boat toward one o'clock as you cut the motor and cast to the fish, which are now at 11 o'clock. Your drift will enable you to maintain a tight line.

Setting the Hook

I like to set the hook with a firm strip strike in all my saltwater fly fishing. When retrieving your fly, always keep the rod low and pointed in the direction of the fly. The fish will often take the fly at such speeds that your normal retrieve will hook the fish before you realize it.

Never use the rod to set the hook. The tip is too soft to drive a large hook into the tough mouth of saltwater game fish. Another advantage of pointing your rod at the fly and strip-striking is that if the fish misses the fly, the fly will still be in the fish's field of view. If a fish doesn't immediately blast off after the hookup, I give it a second strip strike to ensure the hook is firmly set.

Clearing Line to the Reel

When I get on a boat, after greeting the crew and stowing my gear, I survey the casting area. I look for objects that could snag a line and cost me a fish, and possibly some tackle. Most charter captains catering to fly fishers usually rig their boats in a way that makes casting easier. Some of the larger offshore boats that host both conventional fishermen and fly-rodders may have some things to avoid.

If the boat you're on has a fair amount of potential obstacles I suggest you use a stripping basket, a 10-gallon spackle bucket, or a similar item to keep your fly line away from snags. If there is a cleat or something similar in my casting area, I simply toss a wet towel over it. Also watch what you wear; wristwatches, necklaces, even shoelaces can grab your fly line.

The first few seconds after the hookset are critical as the angler tries to clear his line to the reel. Try to forget about the fish—check to make certain the fly line isn't around any part of the boat or your body.

To drive this point home, Captain Al Anderson shared with me an experience he had on an offshore yellowfin trip. Al runs his *Prowler,* a 42-foot North Carolina custom boat with twin diesel engines, out of Snug Harbor and Point Judith, Rhode Island. During the excitement of witnessing dozens of yellowfin busting through his chum slick on one charter, Al inadvertently stepped into a coil of line he had stripped onto the deck.

He was unaware of his predicament until a yellowfin tuna took his fly at 40 mph. Somehow, he cleared the line to the reel but he was unable to step out of the coil, and as the yellowfin quickly ripped off 150 yards of 30-pound Micron backing, the backing cut through his shorts and then his underwear. With tears running down his cheeks from the pain of the line burning through his skin, Al managed to lower the rod and step out of the line. He eventually landed a beautiful 40-pound yellowfin, but he recalls walking funny for quite a few days after that.

Left- or Right-Hand Reeling

Anglers often ask me which hand they should reel with. The answer is simple: You should always reel with your dominant hand. For most anglers, that is the hand they cast with, which means that after hooking a fish and clearing the line to the reel, they would have to switch rod hands. Many anglers don't like to do that while fighting a fish and it's the excuse they use for not reeling with their dominant hand.

Some will argue that there isn't enough time to change rod hands or that doing so is risky during the fight. I disagree. A tuna's first run is long and hard, and there is plenty of time to safely transfer the rod from one hand to the other. The hand you reel with doesn't matter when fighting most fish, but tuna are going to push you to the limit and force you to spend a lot of time reeling against pressure. With tuna you run a greater risk of running out of gas and having your fingers and hand cramp if you don't reel with your stronger hand.

Most anglers learned to fish by keeping the rod in their dominant hand. In fresh water, you don't have to be concerned about your weaker hand being able to reel in a trout or bass. Most saltwater spinning reels are set up for left-handed reeling as well, so the angler casts right-handed and reels left-handed. When these anglers convert to fly fishing they continue the same way. But keep in mind that a spinning reel has a 4:1 or better retrieve ratio. Fly reels have only a 1:1 retrieve ratio, so you're

Reel with your dominant hand.

doing a lot more reeling and your less dominant hand will tire faster, particularly on tough species like tuna.

The Long Battle

After clearing your line to the reel and placing the rod in your less dominant hand, you can enjoy the sound of your drag as the tuna tears off line on one or more of its long, smoking runs. Try to relax and get comfortable, as you are most likely in for a long and grueling struggle, depending of course on the size and toughness of the fish, although I've never encountered a weak tuna.

During the first few blistering runs, point your rod almost directly at the fish, allowing only a slight bend in the rod. This will keep the strain off your back and arms while the drag does its job. During this stage of the battle it is more comfortable for me to slide my hand up on the fighting grip to form a triangle with my arms and back straight; I absorb very little pressure. I frequently place both hands on the rod to relieve strain on my rod hand.

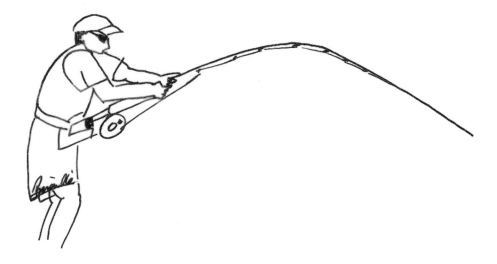

Most first-time tuna anglers get so excited during the fish's early runs that they pull back on the rod for fear that the fish is getting away, straining their backs and arms while trying to stop the tuna. If the fish is still taking line off the reel against the drag, the only thing that pulling back on the rod will do is sap precious energy you'll need later in the fight.

When the fish stops running, particularly if it has taken a lot of line, it's a good idea to ask your captain to slowly move closer to the fish

GENE QUIGLEY

During the tuna's first blistering runs, keep your rod at 45 degrees and let the reel's drag do the work.

while you quickly wind backing onto the spool, making certain to keep tension on the fish. Fly lines stretch, and the closer you are to the fish, the less stretch and the more pressure you can put on a fish.

Fighting fish with your arms will tire you quickly and cause cramping in your arms and hands. When the fish starts to run, drop your arms and rest (remember the triangle) and let the reel's drag do all the work. I have seen powerful men pull with all their might, veins bulging out of their neck and arms, before eventually being forced to quit and hand off their rods to another angler. Keep the rod angle low; this puts greater pressure on the fish from the butt of the rod. The best range of pressure is from the rod almost pointing at the fish up to about 45 degrees.

Keep It Short

After the fish's initial run, it will need to rest. During this critical time you need to be aggressive and apply pressure to close the distance between you and the fish. The longer you let a fish rest before closing the gap, the faster it will recover and be able to prolong the fight.

Try to keep the fight as short as you can, both in terms of time and distance. So many things can go wrong during the struggle, and the longer it lasts the more likely they are to occur. The shorter the battle, the better the chance that the tuna will give out before you and your tackle do. Also, the farther the tuna is from the boat, the less control you have over it. When you're closer, you can apply more pressure.

The angler who is hooked up should concentrate 100 percent of his or her effort on fighting the fish. The rest of the crew should make certain there is no gear or tackle in the angler's way and look for obstructions in the water within several hundred yards of the fish that could snag the line. The most dangerous offshore obstacle is another boat.

I can't tell you how many lines I've seen cut off by the motors of clueless boat operators who troll or speed by another boat, oblivious to the fact that an angler is fighting a fish. I have also seen many tuna lost when the line gets wrapped around lobster pots, buoys, offshore oil rigs, and so on.

Keep the Faith

Eventually the tuna will stop the long, blistering runs away from the pressure and dive deep. Quite often, before going deep it will literally throw you a curve by changing direction and running back toward the pressure, causing your line to go slack. If this happens it's important to keep your composure—and reel like mad! Be confident that the fish is still on; it usually is.

Keep your rod tip low while reeling and *do not* pull the rod back in an effort to see if the fish is still on. If you pull away, you will have to move the rod back toward the fish to continue reeling. This will put even more slack in the line, and that's when you could lose the fish. Have faith that the fish is still on and that the tension from the fly line and backing being dragged through the water will be enough to hold the hook in the fish's jaw.

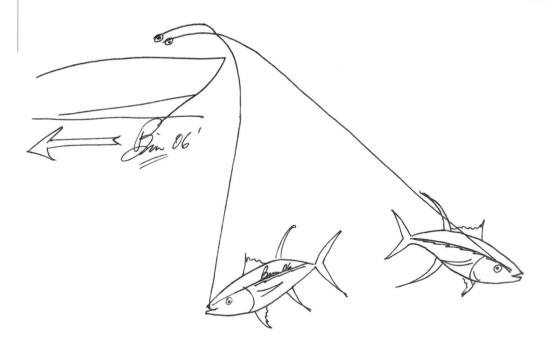

Vertical versus horizontal positioning of tuna during battle

On many occasions I've had experienced captains think I lost my fish due to the lack of bend in the rod. But after 10 or 15 seconds of frantic reeling we would see the rod curve deeply again.

Tug of War

Eventually every tuna battle becomes a vertical tug of war, when the tuna and angler go one-on-one. You can throw modern technology and tackle out the window, because you will be engaged in what feels like hand-to-hand combat. If the fish is a great distance below the boat, have the captain slowly back the boat off so that the fight will become more horizontal, making it easier for you to lift the fish diagonally up through the water column (see illustration above).

Once I have the fly line on the reel, I use my rod hand to pinch it against the cork handle as I lift the fish's head up and start to gain line. Experience and technique will win out over brute strength every time when lifting a big fish. You must get the fish's head up and keep it up. When you do this the fish won't be able to take line, and as it pumps its tail the fight will become circular.

Pretend you are unscrewing the fish from the bottom of the ocean. Lift up and reel down. A slow, steady lift works best. Pump by raising the rod from below horizontal toward a vertical position; but again, never go beyond 45 degrees. The circles will eventually become tight to the boat, and the fish will often start to cross in front of the bow or behind the stern. Resist trying to keep the fish on your side of the boat. Go with it, walking to the bow or stern, and extend the rod so your line clears the boat. This is especially important at the stern, as you need to get your line clear of the engine and propeller.

I've had tuna circle the boat three times or more before I could land them. Doing the tuna shuffle can get chaotic, especially if you have two anglers hooked up and circling at the same time. It gets really crazy when they're going in different directions. If the lines start to cross, go toward the fish; don't try to pull back or the lines will wrap multiple times. If the lines do cross, the best way to remedy the situation is to bring the rod tips together. This will show you which line is over and which is under, enabling you to straighten out the lines and land both fish.

GENE QUIGLEY

After the fish dives deep, pump the rod to gain line.

The Death Spiral

A tuna never gives up, but you can tell you're in control when the fight is reduced to a tight spiral. The fish will have lost most of its ability to run but not the heart and will to win, so it'll keep pumping its tail as you continue to shorten the distance. This is when you can own the fish if you remember one simple rule: Half the spiral is for you and half is for the fish.

When it circles toward you, use its momentum to gain line. When it circles away, drop the rod tip but try not to give line. That is how you close the deal. When the tuna sees the boat, it usually makes one final surge. If you're ready for that and give line as needed, the fish usually burns up its last remaining energy.

Next comes crunch time, when the fish is just about to be landed. This is when many anglers are looking at their fish while trying to move it those last few feet to be landed. It is hard to resist the temptation to move the fish by raising the rod tip. This is known as high sticking, and 9 out of 10 times it results in a broken rod. The best way to move the fish those last critical feet to your partner or guide for landing is to keep the rod parallel to the water and step back, pulling the fish with the rod butt instead of the tip.

Finding Fish

Shrink the Playing Field

Freshwater fish have geological barriers that limit their movements and migrations and thus shrink their playing fields, whether it's a stream, river, or lake. In general, ocean fish are free to roam great distances, with the most limiting factors being water temperature and food supply. The oceans cover 71 percent of our planet, and they average about 2.5 miles in depth. They provide a vast arena for anglers to tackle tuna, especially with a fly rod. As if that immense size didn't offer enough of a challenge, tuna and many of the prey species they feed on are highly migratory. And tides and currents are constantly moving and changing.

To be successful in saltwater fly fishing, you need to fish only the most productive waters during their prime times. I call this fishing the hot spots during their happy hours. You wouldn't go to your favorite drinking establishment at 6 A.M. on a Sunday. But go on a Friday night right after work and you can expect half-price drinks, free finger foods, and lots of happy faces. In many ways, the oceans work the same way, with tides and currents delivering a seafood buffet of prey species to hungry predators at predictable times.

Let's take a look at the many variables that can help you find tuna hot spots and happy hours.

Temperature

The consensus among marine biologists is that ocean temperature is the most important factor in finding fish. This certainly holds true for tuna, which spend a great deal of time in and around the offshore waters of the Gulf Stream. Offshore waters can be divided into two general temperature ranges: warmer, or tropical, and colder, or temperate. Most scientists use 64 degrees Fahrenheit as the dividing line between tropical and temperate.

Tuna spend most of their lives in and around the warm Gulf Stream waters, but unlike most fish, which are cold-blooded, tuna are warm-blooded, enabling them to travel into cooler waters in search of prey. Bluefin can maintain a body temperature higher than any other species of tuna—as high as 35 degrees above the surrounding water temperature. Giant bluefin can withstand colder temperatures than smaller bluefin, which allows them to move into the cold Canadian waters in search of prey. It is unlikely that schoolie bluefin venture much farther north than Cape Cod Bay.

In addition to locating a surface temperature in the correct range, you can increase your chances of finding fish if you can locate an area with sharp boundaries between warm and cool water. For example, if you find an area where the water changes from 68 degrees to 72 degrees in a space of 40 to 50 yards, you have a better chance of finding tuna.

Follow the Stream

The Gulf Stream is a massive ocean river of warm water that flows through the western Atlantic. In some areas it is more than 100 miles wide, and it can be over 1,000 feet deep. Its volume is more than 20 times greater than all the world's rivers and streams combined.

The Gulf Stream begins between Cuba and southern Florida. It flows through the Florida Straits and along the east coast of Florida, where it can be within a few miles of the beach. It then flows northeast, coming close to shore again along the Outer Banks of North Carolina. It comes within 20 miles of North Carolina. By the time it reaches New England it's between 50 and 100 miles offshore. The waters of the Gulf Stream can be more than 15 degrees warmer than the surrounding waters. Bluewater fishing gets its name from the cobalt-blue waters of the Gulf Stream.

Many fish species hunt at the edge of current lines and temperature lines. The front edge of the Gulf Stream provides both a current and a temperature edge, which gathers large accumulations of prey species and provides a conveyor belt of food for predators like tuna. The force of the current moving northeast often causes warm-water ribbons or fingers to break off from the main body of water and move closer inshore. These eddies can be quite large and can last for days and even weeks, providing some excellent nearshore bluewater fishing.

This phenomenon is particularly important to Northeast anglers, since the main body of the Gulf Stream is so far offshore in the north; it is critical for offshore anglers to know where these temperature breaks are located.

Got Bait

Once you've identified an area that has the right temperature ranges for tuna, you need to continue to shrink the playing field within that area. With tuna being such ferocious eating machines, the solution is simple: Find the bait.

Bait concentrations are most frequently found around structure. Structure interferes with flow, causing rips or upwellings that increase current speed and funnel prey species to predators. It can be natural bottom changes like mounds, humps, or offshore canyons or man-made

GENE QUIGLEY

Churning whitewater and seabirds indicate blitzing fish.

objects like shipwrecks, artificial reefs, and oil- or gas-drilling platforms. Several companies produce excellent offshore maps showing all the significant natural and man-made structures. I use maps produced under the name Captain Seagull, which are available at marinas, at fishing shops, and online.

Technology

In the early 1960s, I used to hop on party boats to go offshore fishing for cod. Back then, finding cod hot spots wasn't an exact science. Things were simpler then—not accurate, but simpler. Captains had to rely on a compass to plot direction and estimate distance by how many minutes they were running. And experienced offshore captains really had to know their ecology: Birds, bait, current, weed lines, and position of the sun all were factored into the equation for locating fish.

While knowledge of the ecosystem is still important today, space-age technology has dramatically increased angling success, as well as boating and angling safety. I am mystified by the accuracy of the new Global Positioning System (GPS) devices, which can pinpoint where you are and how to get from point A to point B. Some GPS units come with chart overlays or plotters that allow you to display local navigational charts.

These units can even tell you where you've been in the water and chart it for you. This can be extremely important. Let's say, for example, you have just had great success on a drift and you want to repeat it. The chart will show you where to begin and the direction your drift took. Even inexpensive GPS units have the capacity to store thousands of waypoints. The captain can just hit the "save waypoint" buttons on the GPS unit when an angler hooks up and he'll have stored the latitude and longitude numbers where the fish hit.

Several software programs enable boat owners to transfer GPS data to their personal computers. They can interface those numbers with tides, temperatures, and moon phases to keep incredibly detailed logs, if they're so inclined.

Depth- and fish-finding machines will show the depth and contour of the bottom as well as the presence of prey and predators. Fish finders are sonar (sound navigation and ranging) units that were first developed for the Navy to detect submarines. Probably no piece of equipment has improved the success of offshore fishing as much as a fish finder. A quality unit can pinpoint fish so accurately that I've had sharp-eyed captains predict a fish's strike.

Let's Go Surfing

One of the best pieces of marine electronic gear is actually a personal computer. By surfing the Web, you can find out all kinds of useful information. Getting up-to-the-minute sea surface temperatures and pinpointing temperature breaks, fingers, or pockets of warm water can save you a lot of time and gas when looking for tuna. There are services you can subscribe to that provide this data, but free sites are also available. The better services provide more details, but the free information provided by Rutgers University in New Jersey is quite good (www.marine .rutgers.edu/mrs/sat.data2.html).

Weather reports and current information on water conditions are a snap to get online. Your local TV weatherman doesn't have a clue when it comes to offshore conditions. Before heading out, tap into the marine weather forecast at www.nws.noaa.gov. For even more information about actual conditions on the water, check out the buoy reports. The National Data Buoy Center (www.ndbc.noaa.gov) has buoys that provide up-to-the-minute information on wind speed and direction, air and water temperature, and wave height.

Many fly-fishing Web sites have forums where you can request fishing reports and information, and you usually get fast, accurate responses. My experience has been that the people in these forums are more than willing to share information and answer questions.

Oceans are huge, but fortunately anglers now have plenty of technology to shrink the playing field. A well-equipped offshore boat carries electronic GPS, radar, color video fish finder, VHF radio, autopilot, a sea temperature gauge, and cell phone, in addition to mandatory safety devices such as a life raft, life jackets, flares, horn, fire extinguisher, advanced first-aid equipment, and an emergency position-indicating radio beacon (EPIRB).

Birds as Scouts

Having spent over two decades as president of the New Jersey Audubon Society, I've always been fascinated by the interconnectedness of species in our natural world. Take the unlikely relationship that fish and birds have developed—two of my favorite fauna have given me many a rewarding day at sea.

Many species of seabird follow the migratory routes of baitfish, and seabirds can be a great help to anglers in locating bait and game fish.

What are seabirds? Peter Harrison, author of *Seabirds: An Identification Guide,* defines them as "a species whose normal habitat and food source is the sea, whether they are coastal, offshore, or pelagic." Such species as gulls, terns, cormorants, petrels, shearwaters, pelicans, and gannets would fall under this definition of seabirds.

On a clear day you can see flocks of birds at great distances over the water with the naked eye, but you can increase your likelihood of success by scanning the horizon with a good pair of binoculars. And more and more offshore captains are starting to use their radar units to track seabirds. That's a real testament to how important birds can be in locating fish. A flock of birds has more eyes and can quickly cover more area than an angler can on foot or even in a boat. When birds spot predators pushing bait on top, they do their damnedest to stay with them. Keep in mind that we recreational anglers fish for sport; seabirds fish to survive.

It's important to observe bird behavior carefully, looking for any clues that they are onto something. A bird's sudden turn, change of direction, or dip toward the surface can be a signal that fish are present. Birds flying low and fast are most likely following high-speed fish such as tuna. Birds circling and dropping down over the water are more than likely hovering over slower-moving fish like bass or blues. If birds fly past you or leave to go to another spot it often pays to follow their lead.

While a single bird is not as obvious as a large flock of birds, anglers should be aware that even one bird can broadcast the presence of game fish below. Captain Steve Bellefleur was the first to clue me in to the fact that a lone bird will follow an individual fish, waiting for it to drive bait to the surface. When there is no visible surface action, he has often accurately predicted a hookup by the movement of a single bird that appeared to be shadowing my fly but was actually over the fish.

Learning the important seabird species that frequent your favorite fishing areas will help you predict the size and perhaps even the species of baitfish present. Let's take a look at some of the more common seabirds that can serve as scouts.

The nearshore rips at the mouth of Long Island Sound are a favorite fishing spot of mine. A series of islands squeeze down all the water flowing in and out of the sound, which creates many famous food funnels like the Race, Plum Gut, and the Sluiceway. These islands serve as breeding grounds for thousands of gulls. They also provide some of the most important tern habitat in the world, including the largest breeding colony of roseate terns in North America and one of the largest colonies of common terns in the tristate region. There are so many birds looking for food in this region that it's hard for me to recall a time when I found fish here before the birds did.

It is important for an angler to be able to distinguish between the feeding strategies of gulls and terns. Terns are sleeker and more streamlined than gulls, and they have forked tails and pointed bills. Terns are relatively small seabirds, so they tend to target small baits like silversides, sand eels, and bay anchovy. When terns are actively feeding, it's a good idea to search the water with your smaller flies.

Gulls are trash hounds, typically seen around dumpsters rooting for leftovers. They eat almost anything, and they like their meals big. They feed on crabs in the shallows and have adapted well to our man-made environment, learning to drop clams on hard sand, nearby streets, parking lots, and even the roofs of shore homes to crack open their meal.

Despite their junkyard-dog attitude, they are my favorite scouts. Most species of seabirds can catch fish on their own by diving like a tern or gannet or swimming underwater like a loon or cormorant. Gulls can't dive or swim underwater, so they need predators to drive baitfish to the surface or onto the beach. The presence of feeding terns, gannets, loons, and cormorants indicates the presence of bait, but not necessarily predators. But when you find clouds of tightly packed gulls screaming and flying low over the water, you've hit pay dirt: Gulls signal the presence of prey and predators alike.

Gull identification can be extremely difficult due to the vast number of plumages. It is one of birding's most complex challenges, and I know of several skilled birders that will tell you flat out, "I don't do gulls."

Herring gull

From the angler's point of view, you need to know only two things: Large gulls feed on large baits and small gulls feed on small baits.

Gulls vary greatly in size, as do the prey species they feed on. Large gulls like the great black-backed gull reach a height of 30 inches. They feed on crabs, clams, and bigger baitfish like bunker and herring. At the other end of the scale are the tiny Bonaparte's gull at 13 inches and the little gull at 11 inches. These gulls feed on small baits like bay anchovy and silversides. Down at Harkers Island, North Carolina, during the fall false albacore run, I have seen flocks of Bonaparte's gulls so tight to water over bait balls and busting albies that we couldn't cast toward the fish for fear of hooking these beautiful little birds.

Cormorants are strong underwater swimmers and efficient fish-eating machines. They don't need predators to drive bait to them. They can fish very well on their own. Since they don't need help from predator fish, they aren't reliable game-fish scouts. What you *can* learn from cormorants is the type and amount of bait present.

Study how long they stay underwater on each dive. If it's a short dive, they've most likely caught a fish and bait is likely plentiful. A long dive indicates they are searching for food and bait is likely scarce. Observe these seabirds carefully as they come back up to the surface. You can see and identify the fish they are feeding on as they throw their heads back to swallow them.

Offshore boats can run into a whole suite of pelagic bird species that live out in the open ocean. It wasn't until fairly recently that marine scientists discovered how pelagic birds could survive without fresh water. Their research determined that the birds have glands near the base of the bill that enable them to filter excess salt from their blood. Many pelagic species venture inshore at certain times of year to feed. They are a welcome sight and a rare treat to shore-bound anglers and birders alike.

Northern gannets are most easily identified by their large size. In fact, they are the largest indigenous seabirds in the North Atlantic, running from 34 to almost 40 inches in size, with a wingspan of 65 to over 70 inches. Gannets are high flyers, making them easy to spot at great distances. Immature birds are slaty-brown in color with white spots; adults are all-white with black wingtips.

In the Northeast and Mid-Atlantic, the appearance of large flocks of gannets in the fall usually signals that the herring and bunker runs are in full swing. Gannets follow the bigger baits from the New England coastline to the Outer Banks of North Carolina, as do large schools of big bass and blues. When gannets go on a feeding frenzy, they make

Spotting seabirds like these gannets often leads you to tuna feeding near the surface.

spectacular plunge dives from nosebleed heights. Anglers targeting trophy striped bass from Montauk Point, New York, to Oregon Inlet on the Outer Banks dream of finding a day when it's snowing gannets. That will definitely be a fishing day for the record books.

Offshore tuna boats are always looking for bird activity, especially from the diminutive petrels, which are only 6 to 8 inches in length. Fishermen have nicknamed them "tuna birds," and their sightings are always welcome. These birds seem to dance on the surface looking for small scraps of baitfish that have been devoured by tuna.

A flock of shearwaters hovering over the water is another encouraging sign for the presence of tuna. They are generally solitary animals and gather only when feeding on large quantities of baitfish. When tuna are on small bait the shearwaters follow to wait for them to push bait to the surface. According to Captains Nat Moody and Derek Spengler, who operate First Light Anglers in Rowley, Massachusetts, "Shearwaters equal bluefin tuna."

In addition to birds, other marine life such as whales, porpoises, and sharks can indicate the presence of bait and possibly tuna in the area.

Chum

When there are tuna in waters you can't reach with fly tackle, you can chum or chunk them into range. Several captains described their chumming technique to me as if it were an art form. I won't go that far, but you do need to pay attention when creating a chum slick. You want to keep enough chum in the water to attract and keep the tuna's interest, but not so much that they can hang back deep in the slick and take advantage of a free meal, well out of fly range.

Most marinas sell frozen flats of regionally important baitfish for use as chum. Because the chum doesn't try to escape, tuna can carefully study the bait before deciding whether or not to eat. When this happens, you need a fly that looks like the chum or chunk and you need to drift it naturally back into the slick.

While chumming can be quite productive, drifting a fly back into a slick is not nearly as exciting as casting your fly to a frenzied school of churning tuna. Several charter captains I fish with will net baitfish and carry them in live wells. If tuna aren't showing, they'll anchor and set up a traditional slick. When the tuna are close to the boat they start tossing out the live baits to create a blitz. I have experienced blitzing tuna around the boat for most of the day with live chum. When this happens you'll have multiple hookups and lots of practice doing the tuna tango around the boat.

In several regions, commercial trawlers or draggers create massive chum slicks when they cull their bycatch, which often draws tuna. Those fisheries are covered in detail in the next section.

Chum like these peanut bunkers draws tuna to the surface for fly anglers.

GENE QUIGLEY

Part III

Hot Spots
and
Happy
Hours

Northeast

Football Season

In the spring, my mind turns to thoughts of large striped bass sipping diminutive sand eels and silversides in the shallows. On the new moon in June I'll be stalking the back bays and beach fronts in the wee hours of the morning in hopes of landing a monster bass. Unfortunately, in my home state of New Jersey, bass fishing slows to a crawl by midsummer.

I used to dread those dog days of summer, but now they give me the time to prepare for the upcoming fall "football" season. July will find me tying offshore fly patterns on sharp, heavy wire hooks and tying Bimini loops in my leaders. In August I'll be surfing Web sites, trying to track tuna movements and hot spots.

For me, there is nothing greater in all of sports than getting a group of fellow anglers together and going to a football game. However, our brand of football is a little different; it's played on an aquatic rather than a terrestrial field. While there's no tailgating, if we prepare well there is the real possibility that we will actually get into the game. For extreme hard-core Northeast fly-rodders, this game is about battling small, football-shaped tuna like bonito, false albacore, and skipjack. In recent years, schoolie bluefin tuna have been coming inshore, adding additional spice to our season.

Now before you grab your 10-weight and head to the coast, you should be aware that schoolie bluefin tuna can run over 100 pounds. Bluefin are considered school-sized between the ages of one and a half and six years. These fish range in size from 27 to 59 inches and weigh

Cape Cod Bay has seen a resurgence in schoolie bluefin tuna.

from 15 to 125 pounds. They provide great sport for fly-rodders who want to, as Emeril would say, "kick it up a notch."

While a few bluefin have been caught from shore by spin fishers, I'm not aware of any fly-rodders who have landed a bluefin from shore. Many charter captains feel the most effective way to catch bluefin is by chumming or chunking them into fly-rod range, but there are occasions when you can find them busting bait on the surface. Imagine, if you can, a bluefin tuna half the size of a car crashing through pods of bait at speeds of up to 50 mph. Talk about an adrenaline rush.

Coastal Goes to the Cape

The bluefin tuna gods have been pretty good to me. They have offered me legitimate fly-rod shots almost every time I've targeted bluefin, unlike my quest for yellowfin, and actually let me hook and lose a few just to keep me coming back for more. I landed my first schoolie bluefin tuna on our second annual Coastal Flyrodders trip to Cape Cod.

I was fortunate enough to draw three of the region's top bluefin guides—Captains Joe LeClair, Terry Nugent, and Jaime Boyle—for my three days on the water. Joe and Jaime are dedicated fly fishermen, and although Terry is more comfortable with a spinning rod, he is a ruthless stalker of bluefin tuna. In fact, Terry had gotten me tight to two good-sized schoolie bluefin on a prior trip, but unfortunately neither was landed. Of course, just hooking a bluefin on a fly is an incredibly thrilling feat.

On the first day I was paired with Peter McCarthy and Captain LeClair. Peter planned the trip and is a veteran at this game, with several bluefin battles under his belt, and you'd be hard pressed to find a guide who has put more schoolie bluefin in the boat in the last five years than Captain Joe LeClair. Joe prefers to fish only the bow angler, and Peter was first up in the bow and I was in the stern. Since Peter and I have been chasing inshore tuna together for a number of years, and because I'm a lefty and Peter's a righty we're very compatible tossing flies together.

After watching a few practice shots, Joe was fine with our tossing two lines at the same time. Following a brief search of the waters of Cape Cod Bay for signs of life, we started to see birds working in the distance. In a short time Joe was positioning us upwind from an approaching pod of fish that was busting on peanut bunker.

On our third drift into the school of bluefin, Joe had us in perfect position, and on his command we dropped two fairly accurate shots in front of the churning school. Within seconds we both had fish boiling on our flies. My stomach was in a knot and I held my breath and prayed for an eater. Then I heard Peter scream, "I'm tight! I'm 'bleeping' tight!" As the fish tore off line and Peter's drag began to sing, he turned and with a broad smile said, "Ah, the sweetest sound in all of fishing."

I quickly reeled in to give Peter more room and to photograph the battle. He played the fish skillfully, letting the reel and rod do all the initial work. After three drag-burning runs, Peter got his fly line back on the reel and started to really whip the fish, applying side pressure and using short pumps to gain line. It wasn't long before the fish was circling below the boat. Following Joe's instructions, Peter pumped the rod and gained line as the fish circled toward the boat, then held his ground as it circled away.

As Peter brought the fish toward the surface, Joe told him to keep the rod horizontal and step back. That move brought the tuna into range, and Joe grabbed the leader and drove the gaff into the fish. The entire battle lasted only 25 minutes. I quickly burned a roll of film of Peter with his 40-pound bluefin and took a few digital shots for insurance. There were several other opportunities for bluefin, but only that one fish took a fly that day.

Although I didn't hook a tuna, I did learn a great deal from the captain. Joe pays attention to every detail, and he pointed out that often it's the little things that make the difference, especially at the end of the fight—for example, keeping the rod horizontal and just stepping back to gain those last few feet rather than high-sticking the rod, which places most of the pressure on the tip and often results in a shattered rod and a lost fish.

Extreme Fly Fishing

On our second day, Lenny Maiorano and I were paired with Captain Terry Nugent. This was a good omen, since Lenny and I had been paired with Terry on the second day of last year's trip, when I hooked the two bluefin referred to in chapter 4.

The predominant winds in Cape Cod Bay are southwest, and the bay is protected from these winds by the long arm of Cape Cod. On that second morning of fishing we were greeted by winds coming out of the northwest at 10 knots. The group and crew of guides met at our usual launch site in Barnstable. But launching from Barnstable that morning would've sent us directly into the teeth of the biting wind and 3-foot waves.

After some discussion we decided to trailer the boats around the bay and launch from Plymouth, which would put us in the lee as long as we stayed on the west side of the bay. During the day, the few pods of fish we saw continued to pull us east and away from the protection of land. The winds kept picking up, and four of our boats wisely decided to stay in Cape Cod Bay.

Terry ventured around Race Point with Captains Jaime Boyle and Gene Quigley, and we found numerous pods of fish in the 100-pound range. The combination of wind, waves, and large tuna definitely set the scene for some extreme fly fishing. Despite the rough conditions, the three captains were able to skillfully maneuver their boats to give us some unbelievable fly-rod opportunities.

The wind and waves continued to intensify, and we ended the day skunked and literally beaten and bloody. Our group hooked a total of four fish; all weighed over 100 pounds and three were mercifully lost early in the battles. Matt Spengler had a fish that looked to be just over 100 pounds to the boat before his tippet gave out. His knuckles were bruised and bloodied, having been whacked numerous times by the reel's spinning handle.

Lenny was tossed off the gunwale by a rogue wave and he landed on the deck headfirst, knocking him unconscious momentarily. Luckily he wasn't seriously hurt. To add insult to injury, by the time we left the fish, rounded Race Point, and crossed the rip we were bucking a 25- to 30-knot headwind and pushing right into solid 6-foot seas. We decided that it was too dangerous to make the run across the bay so we tucked into nearby Provincetown Harbor; a 48-foot Viking followed us in due to the harsh conditions.

A Night in P' Town

After we docked, the captains contacted the rest of our group by cell phone to let them know our predicament and to arrange rides back to our vehicles in Plymouth. We knew the wait would be at least an hour, so we wandered into one of the local P' Town bars, the Governor Bradford, to have a few burgers and beers. Boy, did we get more than we bargained for!

Without going into too much detail, I'll mention that it was karaoke night and the local talent included a black female impersonator doing an incredible imitation of Cher. I'm sure the locals found us just as interesting: six wet, windblown, beaten-up anglers wearing rain gear on a windy but very sunny evening. One fellow angler drew quite a bit of attention with his short shorts, white rubber boat boots, long blond hair, and silver reflective sunglasses. In fact, one of the performers did an off-key version of Nancy Sinatra's "These Boots Are Made for Walking" in his honor.

On a Mission

We arrived back at our rental house around midnight and decided to sleep in the next morning and fish the afternoon bite. Joe Pheifer and I would be fishing with Captain Jaime Boyle. After a late breakfast we drove back out to P' Town, where Jaime had moored his boat, the *Boylermaker,* the night before. Joe was driving, I was riding shotgun, and Jaime was in the backseat. Jaime had kind of a cocky smile on his face all morning, and I finally had to ask him why.

"Today I'm on a mission," he said. "Today you're putting a bluefin in the boat . . . that's my mission." That sounded great to me, and I told him I'd do anything I could to help.

We arrived in P' Town Harbor around 10:30 A.M., quickly loaded our gear and lunches onboard, and headed out into Cape Cod Bay. As we left the safety and shelter of the harbor, we could feel the wind pick up. The water was even rougher than the previous day's so we were forced to stay in the bay.

Usually the bite is better on choppy days, but we weren't so lucky. The first few hours were very slow, but we did get one good opportunity. My first cast toward a school of bluefin was way short; I was standing on my fly line. Joe's cast was perfect, landing right in front of the boiling pod of fish, but unfortunately there were no takers.

Things continued to be slow through the middle of the day, with only an occasional flurry. I wasn't that hungry but started lunch out of superstition. It seems like every time I load myself down with sandwiches, chips, and a soft drink, blitzing fish come from out of nowhere and surround the boat for a few seconds—just long enough for me to spill everything—then they're gone.

Even that trick didn't work, and I begrudgingly ate my lunch in relative peace.

You Never Forget Your First

At four o'clock, two of our boats radioed over that they were heading in. We decided to stay as we had noticed a couple of terns starting to work over a few small scattered pods of bluefin, but I knew we were running out of time. By five o'clock, LeClair and Boyle were the last two captains fishing. At 5:30 P.M., well past our normal departure time, we got word that LeClair had Peter McCarthy tight to a fish. I suggested that with the day about over we should go over to photograph Peter's battle and hopefully his fish. But Joe Pheifer and Jaime wouldn't hear of it. Jaime said, "Let's get one more shot."

Shortly after I had accepted Joe's offer of a turn fishing from the bow, Jaime spotted a few fish boiling on the surface. I jumped up into position, stripped off about 70 feet of line, and readied for a cast. Jaime positioned the boat in front of a few terns that were dipping to the surface to pick up scraps the bluefin left behind. He pointed to one of the birds and hollered, "Cast under that bird, I think he's following tuna."

I dropped the fly just in front of the bird and on my second strip I was tight to what felt like a freight train. Since I had made only two strips, clearing line to reel happened in a heartbeat, and instantly the reel started to scream as the fish blasted off. Then, without warning, the fish turned and shot back right at the boat, blasting straight under the center console. I lunged to get the rod from the starboard side around the bow to port, trying to follow the path of the tuna.

PETER MCCARTHY

Captain Jaime Boyle and the author with his first fly-caught bluefin.

For a split second the fish, fly line, and I were all on the same side of the boat. In my haste I had fallen hard onto the gunwale, but with all my adrenaline pumping I didn't feel the pain from my badly bruised ribs. Instead I was focused on the reel's blazing handle, which was hacking away at the sleeve of my rain gear.

As I struggled to free the reel, Jaime screamed, "Watch the motor, watch the 'bleeping' motor!" The fish had changed direction again and my backing was melting off the reel just inches under the blades of the motor. I thrust my rod as deep into the water as I could, staggered back to the stern, and saw that my line had cleared the engine. I stood up as much as my now throbbing ribs would allow, rod firmly in hand and reel screaming as the fish was now some 200 yards to the west of us and showing no signs of slowing down.

At around 250 yards the tuna finally started to tire, and I was able to begin taking back some of my line. The fight became the more traditional give-and-take tuna battle, with me doing most of the giving and the tuna doing most of the taking. I began to have flashbacks of prior battles lost. God, I wanted to land this fish so badly! This was my last chance on the trip, and Jaime and the other guides had worked so hard to get us fish. The bluefin continued to tire and I slowly took control of the fight.

As I got the fly line on the reel, I saw Joe LeClair's boat approaching and I could see that Peter was smiling. It was great to hear that he had landed his fish, but that put even more pressure on me not to screw up. I could see Peter and Ed Janiga taking pictures of the battle, reminding me of the 85-pound tuna I lost boatside the previous year with Captain Terry Nugent. I thought to myself, I've had all the battle shots I want; now I want a hero shot of me with a bluefin tuna.

Suddenly Jaime shouted, "We've got color!" These were the exact same words Terry had used just seconds before I'd lost my fish the year before. I had a lump in my throat so big I couldn't swallow. The tuna took me around the boat one more time, and as I gained the last few feet of line Jaime told me to step back. He grabbed the leader and drove the gaff into the fish. Seconds later a beautiful 46-pound bluefin was in the boat. Jaime smiled broadly and said, "Mission accomplished."

After a round of high fives and a bunch of photos, I sat down, exhausted but ecstatic. Memories of that day still bring a smile to my face. As they say, "You never forget your first."

Hot Spots

The Gulf of Maine is the historic summering grounds for the king of all sport fish, the giant bluefin tuna. These giants have an incredible ability to warm their body temperatures so that they can withstand these cold waters. The smaller schoolie bluefin tuna can't maintain temperatures as high as the adults and therefore don't migrate as far north. The northern limit of school bluefin tuna is usually just north of Cape Cod Bay.

The giants come into the area in early summer, following forage species like herring, mackerel, hake, sand eels, butterfish, peanut bunker, squid, and bluefish. As the water warms, school bluefin begin to show, usually in August or early September. Depending on the weather, they can stay into November.

For the last seven or eight years, light-tackle anglers have been chasing school bluefin tuna in the 50- to 100-pound range. They were present in fishable numbers in all the traditional New England tuna grounds, including Jeffreys Ledge, Stellwagen Bank, Cape Cod Bay, Great South Channel, and an area south of Martha's Vineyard. By all accounts, 2002 was as good as it gets. In mid-August massive schools of baby bunker arrived in Cape Cod Bay, and with them came incredible numbers of school bluefin tuna. These fish had been feeding offshore on mackerel but gladly switched to the slower-moving peanut bunker.

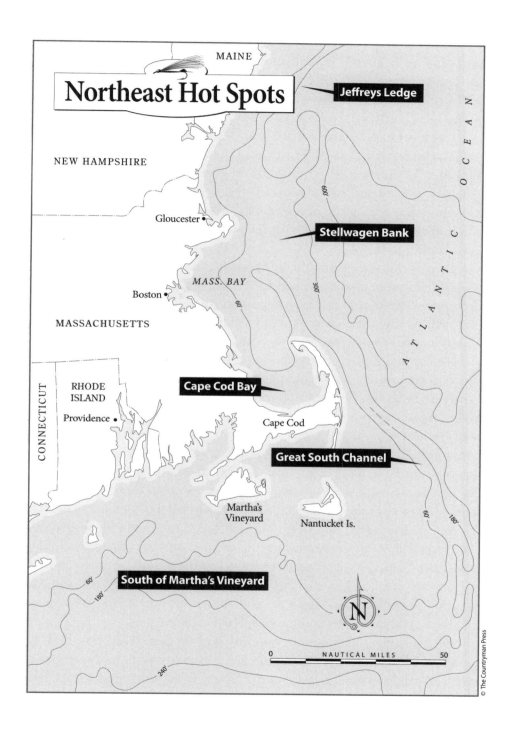

Northeast Hot Spots

Inshore tuna activity of this magnitude hadn't been seen in 40 years, especially on the north shore of Cape Cod. South of Cape Cod there had been small bluefin in recent years off Chatham, south of Block Island, and off Rhode Island, with most of the Rhode Island fish in the 10- to 20-pound range. But 2002 was a banner year off the cape, with large schools of fish in the 40- to 200-plus-pound class at Jeffreys Ledge, at Stellwagen Bank, and in Cape Cod Bay.

Jeffreys Ledge is the northernmost schoolie bluefin tuna hot spot we'll cover in this chapter. The closest port is Gloucester on Cape Ann. Founded by Samuel de Champlain in the early 1600s, Gloucester is America's oldest seaport. For over three centuries, Gloucester fishermen have been harvesting the ocean's bounty. It is still one of the busiest fishing ports on the East Coast, and the fishing fleet supports a major fish-packing industry.

One of the main tourist attractions is the world-famous Man at the Wheel memorial, commissioned in 1923 in memory of the thousands of fishermen lost at sea, and its companion, the Fishermen's Wives memorial. This is the town setting for Sebastian Junger's book, and the subsequent movie, *The Perfect Storm*, which depicts the tragic story about a disaster at sea. This rustic oceanside village has some of the world's best seafood restaurants and a popular tourist attraction in whale-watching.

Gloucester also provides good access to Stellwagen Bank, which is only 14 miles from the harbor. With its accessibility to some of the world's best tuna-hunting grounds, it's no surprise that Gloucester is the largest bluefin fishing port in the world.

Stellwagen Bank is one of the traditional bluefin tuna hot spots, easily accessible from ports on down to Cape Cod. In fact, the southwest corner of Stellwagen is only 5.2 miles off Race Point on Cape Cod. The bank was discovered in 1854 by U.S. Naval Captain Henry Stellwagen. The retreat of massive glaciers during the last ice age formed this underwater sand and gravel plateau, which sits at the mouth of Massachusetts Bay. The plateau is home to a wealth of sea life, from tiny zooplankton to giant humpback and right whales. Bluefin tuna like to travel along the edges and drop-offs common on Stellwagen.

The presence of schoolie bluefin tuna in Cape Cod Bay and the nearshore waters off the cape seems to be a relatively new phenomenon. Most fly anglers found out about the fishery from posts on the Reel Time Web site in 2002, when that fishery just exploded. Daily reports of Cape Cod Bay loaded with fish in early September were common. Captain Joe LeClair, who has been targeting schoolie bluefin tuna for years, says that they have been in the area for eight years or so, but it was a well-kept secret until anglers started posting reports on Reel Time.

The cape wasn't the only area to get a large push of schoolie bluefin in 2002. In mid-July of that year, Gordon's Gully, an area 20 miles south of Wasque Point on Martha's Vineyard, was awash in bluefin, from schoolies up to some 300-pound fish. The gully also gets occasional influxes of skipjack tuna.

The Claw, which lies 25 miles south of Menemsha, is another bluefin hot spot, and in August its waters are usually warm enough to hold skippies, mahi, and sometimes yellowfin tuna. The Star, a hot spot south of the Vineyard, yields bluefin, yellowfin, and skippies. The majority of bluefin south of the Vineyard associated with the trawler discards are juvenile fish in the 15- to 25-pound range.

When I target the nearshore tuna grounds south of the Vineyard I usually fish with charter captains out of Rhode Island, since they're much closer to my home in New Jersey than the Massachusetts guides. I have had the pleasure of fishing with several of the legends in the tuna business. Two of my favorite pioneers in fly-rod tuna fishing, Captains Al Anderson and Dave Preble, hail from Rhode Island.

Anderson is a well-known skipper, author, and lecturer with nearly four decades of experience as a professional charter captain. He is a strong advocate for tagging and catch-and-release fishing. Al has tagged over 4,500 bluefin, and in 2004 he tagged just over 1,000 schoolie bluefin. This was just the second season that he broke the thousand mark; the other was in 1998.

Despite tagging all those fish in 2004, Al claims that today's fishery is a mere shadow of its former self. He reports that back in the early 1960s he could get his clients all the schoolie tuna they wanted on a half-day charter from his 19-foot Aquasport. Al was kind enough to lend me one of his two remaining copies of his landmark book *The Atlantic Bluefin Tuna, Yesterday, Today, and Tomorrow* to help with my research for this publication.

Captain Dave Preble has operated his charter boat, the *Early Bird*, out of Snug Harbor, Rhode Island, for over 20 years. Dave and his family have a long seafaring tradition, including an ancestor, Ed Preble, who commanded the USS *Constitution* during the Barbary War off northern Africa. Dave is also a noted author, having written several books on offshore fishing, including *Fly Fishing Offshore: Cape Cod to Cape Hatteras* and *Sport Fishing for Yellowfin Tuna*, in which he describes his pioneering work on fly fishing for yellowfin.

August and September usually find Dave and Al with their clients chasing school bluefin tuna in an area known as the Mud Hole 20 miles south-southeast of Point Judith, Rhode Island, and 8 miles east of Block Island. The Mud Hole can be described as a channel or trench that runs northeast for about 14 miles. It's about 215 feet deep in an area that averages only 125 feet.

This area is a popular place for the commercial fishing fleet to drag their nets. These draggers are the key to the Rhode Island schoolie bluefin fishery. When they pull their nets in they lose a certain percentage of their catch overboard and then they cull out the fish they can't sell. Both Dave and Al commented that bluefin tuna are extremely smart animals that know the draggers will supply a generous and easy meal.

Bluefin are attracted to these ships by the noise their metal nets make dragging over the bottom of the ocean, responding like Pavlov's dogs even before cull is present. When the draggers are towing, the tuna follow in anticipation of a food fest.

The trick is for the angler to get in the wake of the draggers and set up a chum slick to intercept the tuna. If you find a dragger culling, you most likely will have hit the mother lode of feeding tuna. The cull will be floating down-current from the trawler, so it's a good idea to bring a net and scoop it up. The floating cull usually includes whiting and hake, which you can use as chum to keep the tuna happy and within fly-rod range.

Another hot spot is an area known as the Dump. It's about twice as far offshore as the Mud Hole, but it offers longfin albacore, skipjack, and yellowfin tuna. The Dump is roughly a 40-mile run from Rhode Island and 50 miles from Montauk, New York. Both Dave and Al have caught numerous yellowfin on flies off Rhode Island, but they caution that the conditions have to be perfect. You need a bubble of warm, clear water to come in off the Gulf Stream, and some years this happens for only a few days.

Offshore Canyons

Most of my tuna fishing in New England is inshore, where it's not uncommon to catch schoolie bluefin, bonito, little tunny, and even skipjack tuna. Fly anglers who go farther offshore can add yellowfin and longfin albacore to the list. While I haven't fished the canyons off New England, I do follow the weekly fishing reports. In recent years both Veatch's and Hydrographer canyons produced excellent catches of yellowfin and longfin albacore for conventional anglers. On a recent trip to

Veatch's Canyon, Captain Terry Nugent reported yellowfin and longfin tuna busting through his chum line well within fly-rod range.

Depending on your port of departure, the canyons are between 80 and 125 miles offshore. That's a long run for a day, so I would strongly recommend an overnight or multiday trip. I'm not aware of any such trips run exclusively for fly fishing, but I'm sure if you got a group together you could charter a crew.

Naturals and Their Imitations

In the Northeast tuna feed on a variety of prey species, everything from bluefish weighing in the teens to tiny krill. High on their menu are Atlantic herring, sand eels, silver hake, bunker, mackerel, and squid. For killer fly patterns, most guides turn to three expert tiers—Dave Skok, Rich Murphy, and First Light Anglers.

When tuna are on peanut bunker, tinker mackerel, or silversides, I'll fish Skok's Mushmouth. It is incredibly realistic looking and very durable and won't foul. Although I've been tying flies for almost 40 years, thoroughly enjoy it, and am reasonably proficient at the vice, the Mushmouth is one of two flies I won't tie. My reasoning is simple. The most important piece of equipment you have is a fly—if your flies don't look and fish right, nothing else matters. I can't tie a Mushy nearly as well as Dave, so I buy mine from him.

The other pattern I don't tie is Joe Blados's floating Crease Fly. Joe Darcy, one of my fishing partners, is a master at turning out Crease Flies in various shapes, colors, and sizes, and I can't match the quality of his flies. There is no greater thrill than to see a tuna chase down a Crease Fly, slashing through the surface at speeds over 40 mph.

Captains Derek Spengler and Nat Moody of First Light Anglers in Rowley, Massachusetts, are two of the pioneers of flyrodding for bluefin tuna in the Northeast. They developed a generic baitfish pattern that can be tied in various shapes and sizes to match the prey species the tuna are targeting. The fly has a rabbit-strip tail, a body made with Kinkey Fiber, and a tungsten cone head. By design, the fly never stops moving in the water. The weight in the cone head makes it dart up on the strip and dive down on the pause, and the rabbit tail is constantly moving.

Captain Joe LeClair, one of the top tuna guides in the Northeast, rates Rich Murphy's Pamet River Special as the number-one tuna fly. This is his go-to fly when the tuna are on sand eels and small peanut bunker.

Mid-Atlantic 10

Spooled

Like the Northeast, the Mid-Atlantic region has seen an explosion of in-shore schoolie bluefin tuna in recent years. Captain Joe "Maz Man" Mustari related a day on the water that every fly fisher dreams about. He was fishing with his father and a few friends aboard Mark Sherman's 42-foot Bertram at the Bacardi wreck about 75 miles off New York Harbor.

He described it as a calm September day with glass-flat water. Scallop boats were working the area and bluefin tuna were feeding in the slicks behind the boats. Joe and his crew were able to successfully chum the tuna away from one of the scallop boats with peanut bunker. It wasn't long before they had hundreds of schoolie bluefin boiling on the surface right behind Sherman's boat, gobbling up peanut bunker and Crease Flies as fast as the crew could throw them into the water.

One by one they hooked up as their flies hit the water, and for the next six hours they were doubled and tripled up on bluefin in the 15- to 30-pound range. At one point they actually had five fly rods tight to tuna.

After about three hours of landing small fish, Joe hooked one that burned off 200 yards of line in just a few seconds. The others knew he was into a good fish and reeled in their lines to give him room. After several long runs the tuna sounded deep. Being an experienced angler, Joe knew how to pressure it, and by skillfully pumping the rod he took control of the fight and began to close the distance between the tuna and the boat.

Soon his fly line was back on the reel and the fish was just 50 feet below the boat doing the tuna spiral. Joe was gaining line on every pump and his partners were ready with the net, but no one was ready for what came next.

On the very next pump the pressure caused the spool to pop out of the reel, and it bounced off the gunwale and into the drink. The quick-thinking crew grabbed the backing and frantically started to pull the spool back to the surface. It was difficult to retrieve because the line continued to unwind on every pull, but with two fellows pulling hand over hand they were able to make small gains. With about 100 yards of backing lying on the deck, the spool was finally close enough to reach with the net.

All this time Joe had been fighting the fish by pinching the fly line against the rod's cork handle. The rescued spool was put back on the reel and miraculously Joe was able to reel in all of the backing while still fighting the tuna. Just minutes later, they landed a beautiful 75-pound bluefin tuna, a great reward for all their efforts.

Joe and his group lost count of the number of tuna they landed that day, but the fishing was still going strong when the five weary anglers quit from exhaustion and left for shore with the fish still feeding.

Mark Sherman and Captain Joe Mustari show off a bluefin tuna caught 75 miles off New York Harbor.

The Good Old Days

The Mid-Atlantic region has a long tradition of recreational angling for tuna, especially bluefin. In the early 1930s they were the most important big-game species in the region. The main reason for their popularity was the relatively short distance one had to travel to catch them compared to other big-game species.

Their popularity continued for decades, and by the early 1960s schoolie bluefin tuna were the region's premier inshore game fish. As a youngster, I remember reading reports of anglers trolling within sight of the beach and finding schools of small bluefin tuna that stretched for miles. They were the bread and butter of the inshore charter and small-boat industries, as well as the economic backbone for dozens of small port towns.

According to charter captain and outdoor writer Al Ristori, "Trolling for school bluefin tuna used to be the mainstay of the summer charter-boat industry, until seiners sponsored by the old Bureau of Commercial Fisheries destroyed the superabundant stocks within a few years." I have heard estimates of as many as 100,000 recreationally landed school bluefin tuna per year in New York and New Jersey during the heyday of that fishery. By the mid-1970s, the purse-seine industry had harvested tremendous numbers of school bluefin.

Due to concerns about the declining population of bluefin, in 1975 the Atlantic Tunas Convention established the first harvest limits for recreational anglers at four school bluefin per angler, per day. Imagine how good the fishing must have been when the limit imposed was four fish per angler. Still, the once abundant fishery didn't last long thanks to overfishing by purse-seine boats, which all but eliminated the inshore school bluefin fishery from the late seventies until early in this century.

During most of 2004 and 2005, the nearshore waters from Virginia all the way to Cape Cod were blessed with warm-water temperature breaks that came in off the Gulf Stream. With the warm water came tons of baitfish, and the combination gave us an inshore schoolie bluefin fishery that was unparalleled in recent memory. Most of the fish weighed between 15 and 40 pounds, the ideal size for fly fishing. Hundreds of tuna virgins got their first bluefin on flies, and in 2005 three women's tippet-class IGFA world records were set.

Have the good old days returned? We'll all have to wait for the 2006 tuna season to find out. Hopefully these fish will escape seiners' nets and long-liners' hooks and return in good numbers.

Canyon Country

In addition to the recent revival of the inshore tuna bite, our offshore canyons come alive every summer with incredible numbers of pelagic fish species. When the warm-water eddies from the Gulf Stream spin off and come into our deepwater canyons, we're blessed with a world-class tuna fishery. From July to November the canyons can give up fly-rod bluefin, yellowfin, skipjack, and longfin albacore.

The canyons lie at the edge of the continental shelf, which is the submerged portion of our coastal plain. It extends eastward about 80 miles to the 100-fathom line. As the shelf ends, the water depth drops from about 600 feet to 6,000 feet in a mere 10 miles along the continental slope. The shelf edge is cut by numerous steep-sided gorges called submarine canyons. Like their land counterparts, they were cut by swiftly flowing rivers. From Montauk, New York, to Virginia's Eastern Shore there are about a dozen canyons, and they all host tuna for at least a portion of the season.

The granddaddy of all the Mid-Atlantic canyons is the Hudson Canyon. It is unquestionably the number-one offshore hot spot on the entire East Coast, both in terms of the number of boats that fish it and the number of fish it gives up. The Hudson River starts as a tiny little trout stream in the Adirondack Mountains in upstate New York and becomes a major river as it flows to New York Bay some 275 miles from its source. The Hudson Canyon continues along a 500-mile underwater valley with precipices a mile deep in the ocean floor.

The Hudson is in effect a drowned river dating back to the last ice age, and it is geologically similar to the Grand Canyon. If you're planning to fish the Hudson or any of the Mid-Atlantic canyons, I suggest you book an overnight trip. Depending on your port of departure, the canyons off New York and New Jersey are anywhere from 80 to 100 miles offshore, while Delaware, Maryland, and Virginia have access to canyons that are as close as 40 to 50 miles offshore.

Long-Range Fishing

Long-range bluewater has seen very little fly-rod activity in the Atlantic, unlike the West Coast. In the late 1980s Captain Gene Berger started organizing overnight canyon trips, which continued for about a decade. For years Captain Gene Quigley has been putting his clients into false albacore, bonito, bluefin, and skipjack tuna from the inshore and mid-range hot spots off New Jersey.

Gene has been fishing the offshore canyons for over two decades and now is one of the few East Coast skippers offering overnight fly-fishing trips, giving his anglers shots at yellowfin and longfin albacore as well. On the overnight trips Gene uses a spreader light behind the boat to draw squid to the surface. He reports that on a good night it's not uncommon to have several dozen squid being chased around the stern by hungry tuna.

Surface-feeding tuna are a rare sight in this region, so most of the offshore fishing is done by finding fish and then chunking or chumming them to the surface. The most common bait for chunking in the canyons is cut butterfish. The challenge with chunking is that the tuna often lie back in the slick, and they can become very selective.

For these conditions, Gene has developed a series of very realistic chunk flies. When that doesn't work he tosses live bait for chum, and that always seems to fire up the tuna. He points out that it is important to spread the chum all around the boat, since chumming in the same spot allows the fish to feed deeper in the slick. He also cautions that any pause in chumming could lose the school.

Chumming is effective in the Mid-Atlantic region's offshore waters.

Hot Spots

New York and New Jersey

Montauk sits at the eastern tip of Long Island and is home to one of the largest recreational fleets on the entire East Coast. There is a sign on the way to this great fishing hub that reads, "Welcome to Montauk, Fishing Capital of the World." More IGFA world records have come from Montauk than any other place on the East Coast. In addition to party boats and well over one hundred charter boats, Montauk has everything a visiting angler could want: tackle shops, accommodations for every budget, and some great seafood restaurants.

Boats out of Montauk can target hot spots like the Mud Hole, the Dump, Jenny's Horn, Ranger Wreck, and the Butterfish Hole. The inshore false albacore run in the fall has captured the attention of fly-rodders from around the globe, and bluefin tuna can and do pop up anywhere from just off the beach out to the 100-fathom line at this time. Boats fishing out of the inlets farther west on Long Island and from northern and central New Jersey can target the Texas Tower/Bacardi/Bidevind triple-wreck area southeast of Fire Island and the Tip and East Elbow areas of the Hudson Canyon.

The Hudson Canyon is a long, deep trench with a series of lumps, holes, ridges, and wrecks. The nearshore lumps and wrecks and ridges between the 15- and 30-fathom lines provide a great inshore bluefin bite. As the Gulf Stream settles into the offshore canyons, warm eddies spin off and enter the nearshore waters and hot spots like the Monster Ledge, Oil Wreck, Little Italy, and the Glory Hole. During the summer and early fall, these eddies deliver bait and pelagic fish species, and anglers can expect to have shots at skipjack, false albacore, bonito, and school-sized bluefin tuna, an inshore tuna grand slam. As the fall progresses, giant bluefin can be found in the Mud Hole and the Glory Hole.

Cape May sits at the southern tip of New Jersey. In fact, it's south of the Mason-Dixon Line. Its strategic location gives charter captains access to southern New Jersey hot spots and those off Delaware, Maryland, and Virginia. This town is not only a great port to fish from but also a great place to bring the family for vacation. A sampling of activities would include whale-watching, playing the slots in Atlantic City, walking the boardwalk, or going on the amusement rides in Wildwood.

Cape May is also a world-class destination for watching birds in migration. It is the site of the largest hawk migration in North America and hosts the second largest concentration of shorebirds in the Western Hemisphere. There are a variety of accommodations here, and the fresh seafood is out of this world.

For tuna anglers, the offshore canyons provide yellowfin, longfin, and bluefin action all summer and well into the fall. Popular spots include Toms and Lindenkoehl canyons. From Cape May you can also make the run southeast to fish Wilmington, Baltimore, and Washington canyons.

Delaware, Maryland, and Virginia

Delaware and Maryland charters target yellowfin and bluefin tuna at the Fingers, which lie 35 miles southeast of the Indian River inlet. Other popular tuna areas include Massey's Canyon, which lies 38 miles southeast of Indian River inlet, and the Hot Dog Canyon located 40 miles off the inlet. In early July 2005, the Hot Dog produced a true giant. David Collins landed an 873-pound bluefin tuna, besting the state record by over 500 pounds. The earlier record was a 322-pound bigeye tuna.

Ocean City, Maryland, claims to be "the White Marlin Capital of the World," and while that's a stretch, it certainly can be rated the number-one white marlin area on the East Coast. Due east of Ocean City, between the 20- and 30-fathom lines, is a 20-mile stretch of humps and lumps that holds massive schools of sand eels. In spring the bluefin move into this

GENE QUIGLEY

An angler ready to take a shot behind a scallop boat

area when the water temperature rises above 62 degrees, and they stay there until it reaches the low 70s, when they move into deeper water. The Hot Dog and nearby lumps are very reliable schoolie bluefin hot spots, and their proximity to deep water can provide yellowfin on occasion.

Boats out of Wachapreague Inlet, Virginia, target yellowfin and bluefin in an area know as the Lumpy Bottom (Chunky Bottom to the locals). From Virginia up to Cape May, the tuna bite can be spectacular behind working scallop boats.

Naturals and Their Imitations

The Mid-Atlantic region has quite a variety of prey species for tuna to feed on. Some of the more predominant critters include butterfish, bay anchovy, silversides, peanut bunker (menhaden), herring, sand eels, tinker mackerel, and squid. When the scallop boats are working, especially when the crew is opening the shells and tossing scallop guts overboard, bluefin follow to gorge themselves on the guts and anything else that comes into the slick.

The Mid-Atlantic region also has a plethora of great fly tiers, including Bob Popovics, whom Lefty Kreh calls "the most innovative tier I have ever known." With so many good tiers, local fly shops and guides offer anglers a wide assortment of "match the hatch" patterns.

For the smaller prey species like silversides and bay anchovy, you can't go wrong with Popovics's Surf Candy and Deep Candy. When tuna

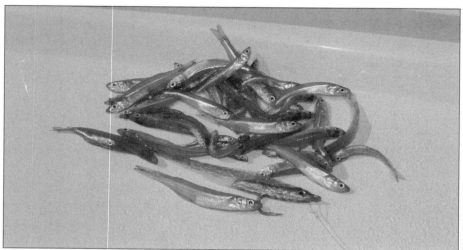

TOM GILMORE

Silversides surround a Popovics Surf Candy fly.

are chasing sand eels, Bob's Jiggy and Clouser's Deep Minnow are the go-to flies. Like the Deep Candy, both the Jiggy and Deep Minnow incorporate weight at the front of the hook. This makes them dart up on the strip and dive down on the pause. These flies never stop moving, which makes them incredibly effective. I incorporate weight to achieve this same action on most of the patterns I tie.

In addition to an arsenal of Popovics's classics, I also carry several of the innovative offshore patterns developed by Captain Gene Quigley. For the wider profile baits like butterfish or peanut bunker, I use a Lefty's Deceiver–type pattern like Gene's Flash Butterfish or Popovics's Bucktail Deceiver. When you are chunking tuna into fly range, Gene's Butter Chunk pattern or his Marabou Head Chunk will usually produce strikes. Always the innovator, Gene has developed a scallop-gut pattern that has worked well for him behind the scallop boats.

For squid flies, again I turn to Popovics and Quigley; both Popovics's Shady Lady Squid and Quigley's Tuna Squid are reliable producers.

Southeast 11

In this chapter we'll explore fly fishing for tuna from the Outer Banks of North Carolina to the Florida Keys. Tuna spend a great deal of time traveling in and around the warm waters of the Gulf Stream. As the Gulf Stream flows out of the Gulf of Mexico it is closest to shore along the Florida Keys and just off Palm Beach in southeast Florida. The stream then flows northeast and comes close to shore again off the Outer Banks of North Carolina. So it should come as no surprise that if you ask me where to target tuna in the Southeast, the Outer Banks or the Florida Keys would be my answer.

Outer Banks

For decades, North Carolina has had a reputation as one of the best surf fisheries anywhere in the world. Northeastern surf casters have long made late-fall trips to the unspoiled beaches of the Outer Banks to extend their fishing seasons and to try their luck at catching trophy channel bass, giant bluefish, and jumbo striped bass. The surf of the Outer Banks has produced three all-tackle world records: a 31-pound 12-ounce bluefish; a 94-pound 2-ounce red drum; and a 13-pound Spanish mackerel.

My first tuna fly-fishing trip to the Outer Banks was in November of 1995, and the tuna we targeted were false albacore. My trip was motivated by an article by Tom Earnhardt in *Fly Fisherman* magazine. Tom is the author of *Fly Fishing the Tidewaters,* and he introduced me and the rest of the world to the great false albacore run off Harkers Island. I can still vividly remember Tom's description of a false albacore's blistering run as "tuna melt."

Tom had been quietly targeting the Outer Banks false albacore run since the early 1980s. Back then they were considered a trash fish on the Outer Banks, and with the wealth of good-eating fish available, the locals felt it would be foolhardy to fish for albies. That attitude changed when Tom came out of the closet and introduced a group of outdoor writers to this great fishery in 1994. Articles started appearing in popular fishing magazines, and it wasn't long before anglers started coming to Harkers Island from the Northeast, where false albacore and bonito have a cultlike following.

Word of this great fishery spread like wildfire, and fly-rodders from around the country and around the world started making annual pilgrimages to the tiny hamlet of Harkers Island. Needless to say, the economic boost visiting anglers gave this region during its traditional off-season was not lost on the locals, who developed a whole new respect for false albacore.

"Creature" Breaks the Century Mark

Around the time false albacore were getting popular off the southern Outer Banks, veteran offshore charter Captain Steve "Creature" Coulter and a few of his extreme fly-fishing clients began exploring a whole new frontier. They were starting to target bluefin tuna in excess of 100 pounds using IGFA-class tippets.

According to Steve, his main motivation was the fact that the other charter captains said it couldn't be done. After all, at that time no one on the planet had recorded landing any species of tuna over 100 pounds on a fly. In fact, up to 1996, the fly-rod bluefin record was 53 pounds, taken by angler Everett A. Petroni Jr., and the largest fly-rod tuna was an 81-pound yellowfin landed by Jim Lopez.

Steve and his fellow anglers were entering uncharted waters and testing the limits of their tackle as well as their stamina and determination. On January 23, 1996, the very first day that Steve and Maryland angler Mike Reid set out to break the bluefin tuna record, they broke it twice. The first fish was 85 pounds and the second weighed 128 pounds, which became the first fly-caught tuna weighing over 100 pounds to be entered into the IGFA record books. Mike was using an 18-weight rod and a 650-grain shooting head, and the grueling battle lasted over two and a half hours.

Equally remarkable was Raz Reid's (no relation) IGFA 16-pound tip-pet record. Raz had booked two days with Steve with a goal to be the first angler to land a 100-pound bluefin on a fly, and he had invited a friend, Captain Brian Horsley, to come along. Mike Reid and Steve had broken the 100-pound mark just a few weeks before this trip.

Early on the first day, Raz hooked two fish estimated to be in the 300-pound range that quickly broke off. Later in the day he hooked a potentially landable fish they estimated at just over 100 pounds. After an epic battle that lasted almost three hours, Raz landed an 85-pound bluefin—an awesome fish on 20-pound class tippet, but not the 100-pound monster he was looking for.

On the second day, despite the grueling battle the day before, Raz was still game to try to land a 100-pound tuna. It didn't take long for him to hook up again, and for the first two hours the battle was reminiscent of the previous day—a few long, screaming runs followed by the vertical tug of war. Well into the third hour, Raz told his crew that he thought the fish was actually getting a little stronger. That's when an angler really has to be mentally and physically tough.

Raz was up to the test, and it paid off. After almost four hours the mate, Ken Dempsey, drove the gaff into the shoulder of the tuna. When the fish was safely in the boat, Raz revealed that he had switched from a 20-pound to a 16-pound class tippet. The fish weighed 101.5 pounds, beating the old 16-pound class tippet record by an astonishing 86.5 pounds!

From 1996 to 2000, the five largest fly-caught tuna in the world came from Coulter's boat, and they were all bluefin. Steve's strategy was to look for a school of bluefin that had fish small enough to tackle with fly outfits and chunk-feed them until they surfaced within casting range. Imagine how exciting it would be to see a school of 100-pound-plus tuna boiling on the surface and eating chunks and flies 40 feet off the stern of your boat.

Large concentrations of medium and giant bluefin tuna gather every winter off Cape Hatteras and south to Morehead City, North Carolina. Most years they start showing up in late autumn and can stay into April, with January through March being prime time. The fishing can be so reliable that conventional-gear charters can land up to two-dozen fish per day.

These fish are often caught in relatively shallow water east and south of Cape Hatteras around wrecks and man-made reefs. Another hot spot is along the edge of the Cape Lookout shoals, which are about 15 miles off Morehead City. Here bluefin are taken in water that is as shallow as 45 feet, and while I have no desire to experience the pain and suffering of tackling a giant or even a medium bluefin tuna on a fly, this would definitely be the place to do it—and someone did.

In the fall of 2000, while working on a draft of my book *False Albacore,* I noted then that "new innovations in tackle and technique would raise the world-record bar on all species of tuna." In hindsight this was quite an understatement.

On Friday, January 12, 2001, angler Brad Kistler took fly fishing for tuna to a whole new level. Fishing a wreck off the Cape Lookout shoals aboard Captain Bill Harris's boat *Fly Caster,* Kistler landed a 196-pound 9-ounce bluefin, shattering Stephen Hutchins's record by an astounding 67 pounds. Just as astounding is the fact that he landed the fish in 75 minutes using a Sage RPLX 8-foot 9-inch, 14-weight rod, Charlton 8550 reel, and 20-pound class tippet. Now that's what I call extreme fly fishing.

North Carolina is a feeding region for large prespawn fish, with spawning fish going to the Gulf of Mexico or the Mediterranean Sea. Scientist Dr. Barbara Block runs her Tag a Giant research project out of Morehead City every winter. If you want to catch a giant and help scientists discover more about these magnificent creatures, you can contact Dr. Block at www.tunaresearch.org. The tag-and-release fishing utilizes heavy conventional tackle to keep the fight short and thus increase the likelihood of the fish's survival.

Bluefin aren't the only tuna that anglers are setting records with on the Outer Banks. Several women's world records for yellowfin have been broken in recent years. In the fall of 1999, Theresa Hutchins set the women's fly-rod world record with a 39-pound yellowfin taken on 20-pound tippet, and less than three weeks later she broke the 16-pound class-tippet record with a 16-pound yellowfin. On the first trip, her husband, Steve, landed six yellowfin tuna up to 50 pounds on fly-rod poppers. Both trips were with Captain Brenner Park on his boat *Smoker* out of Oregon Inlet.

Fly fishing for yellowfin tuna, as with bluefin, is gaining in popularity, with more that half the class-tippet records being set since 1998. On October 21, 2001, fishing out of Oregon Inlet, Theresa Hutchins broke her own world record 20-pound class tippet with a 43-pound 8-ounce yellowfin. Less than two months later, she went back out with her hus-

BRIAN HORSLEY

Captain Sarah Gardner's 20-pound tippet-class world-record yellowfin (53 pounds 4 ounces), taken off the Outer Banks.

band, Steve, aboard Captain Cliff Spencer's *Anticipation* and broke her 16-pound class-tippet record with a fish weighing 55 pounds 8 ounces.

The next day Captain Sarah Gardner landed a 53-pound 4-ounce yellowfin—a new 20-pound tippet-class world record. Sarah was fishing off Hatteras Inlet with her husband, Captain Brian Horsley, and Raz Reid on the *Sea Creature,* captained by Steve "Creature" Coulter. The group fished 13- and 14-weight rods to schools of 50- to 80-pound tuna blasting through butterfish chunks.

The Rest of the Fishery

Yellowfin tuna are the mainstay of the charter fleet out of Oregon and Hatteras inlets. Good catches of yellowfin can occur at any time of year, but most years, the late fall–early winter fishery is fantastic, with daily limits being the rule, not the exception. The fish generally don't run as big here as they do in the Florida Keys and throughout the Gulf of Mexico, ranging from 15 to 100 pounds.

The Gulf Stream is located about 35 miles southeast of Oregon Inlet and 35 miles east of Hatteras Inlet. Fishing is usually best in the blended water, where green inshore water mixes with the bright blue waters of the Gulf Stream. Charter captains target a 35-mile stretch of the Gulf Stream from an area called the Point to the Diamond Shoals Light Tower. Most of the time, you won't find Outer Banks yellowfin near the surface, so the best strategy is to troll until you find a school and then chunk them into fly-rod range.

Blackfin tuna are found in the warm waters of the Gulf Stream off the Outer Banks from April to November, but they are most prevalent in the warmer months of June through September. If you want to really get into some serious blackfin fishing, the best locations are the Florida Keys and the Gulf of Mexico.

Bermuda

The island of Bermuda sits in the Atlantic about 600 miles east of the Carolinas. It is almost completely overlooked by fly fishers, but it shouldn't be. Its spring yellowfin tuna run rivals that of any other tuna destination. Natural corals built on top of inactive volcanoes formed the island and the nearby Challenger and Argus banks, which are a continuation of those volcanic peaks. They rise up dramatically from the ocean floor from over 600 fathoms to approximately 30 fathoms in a matter of a few hundred feet. This creates upwellings and food funnels, and the tuna feed in these currents.

To date, there have been very few fly-rod anglers plying Bermuda's offshore tuna waters. That will change as anglers learn of the success of the Bermuda Fly Fishing Invitation, a new bluewater event hosted by angling personalities Flip Pallot and Bob Brien. The first invitational was held in 2004 and the fishing was tremendous, with 12 anglers hooking and landing 72 yellowfin in four days of fishing. The fish ranged from around 35 pounds to just over 60 pounds.

According to Captain Keith Winter, the fishing was just as good during the 2005 event. Keith reports being able to chum the yellowfin right to the transom and says that anglers could literally pick out the tuna they wanted to catch. The action starts toward the end of April and can last into July.

Depending on the conditions, charter captains anchor or drift, using chum or chunks to bring the fish into range. Once tuna get into the slick, Captain Joey Dawson has figured out a clever way to get them to the surface. He tosses a few frozen anchovies out to bring the fish on top, as frozen baits ride higher in the water column than thawed baits. To increase the likelihood of a fly angler getting hooked up, Captain Dawson quickly works a hookless MirrOlure through the chum slick to get the tuna fired up.

Unlike most yellowfin hot spots, Bermuda's tuna waters are only a short boat ride from the docks, giving the angler much more fishing time. The Challenger and Argus banks are located 11 and 18 miles, respectively, off the southwest end of the island.

Florida Keys

The Florida Keys are a famous destination for many saltwater game fish. The inshore flats around the keys offer world-class fly fishing for tarpon, permit, and bonefish, and the nearshore bluewater fishing for billfish is also world-class.

But when it comes to blackfin tuna, the keys are in a class by themselves, considering that both the IGFA all-tackle and the IGFA fly-rod world records both come from the keys. If you think they were flukes, consider that 14 of the 18 line-class world records and 8 of the 10 tippet-class world records come from the keys. It's no wonder that

JIM LEVISON

The author getting ready to release a false albacore in Florida anglers have dubbed the offshore waters around Islamorada and Marathon "Tuna Town."

Middle Keys

The famed Alligator Light stands just offshore of Islamorada, and it's the starting point for the large fleet of sportfishers that target blackfin tuna every spring over underwater seamounts. There are four natural seamounts in the area: Islamorada Hump, 409 Humps, Key Largo Hump, and the Marathon or West Hump. In addition, there are several wrecks large enough to act like seamounts. These humps lie between 12 and 22 miles offshore, so it's only a short run to the blackfin tuna grounds. This is a mixed blessing, because the humps can get quite crowded during the peak of the tuna season. It's best to fish early or late in the day.

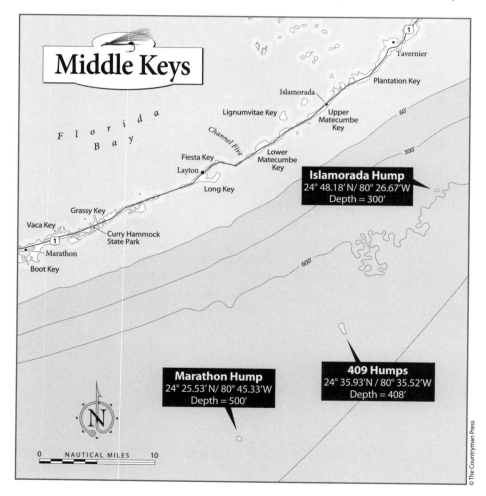

The humps rise several hundred feet from the floor of the ocean. When you combine their height with the strong current of the Gulf Stream flowing northeast over them at a rate of 2 to 3 knots, you have a large upwelling pushing baitfish in the rips that form on the northeast side of the humps.

The *Spiegel Grove,* a recently scuttled 510-foot freighter that sank in 125 feet of water off Key Largo, creates the same rips and bait funnels as the natural seamounts. The state has attached eight mooring balls to the freighter's deck, which allows boats to remain safely over the freighter without anchoring. Blackfin can be found offshore all along the Florida Keys year-round, with the best action peaking in the spring when blackfin feed reliably and voraciously.

Key West

Blackfin are the most common tuna around Key West and they are available year-round. They tend to school around wrecks in the spring, which is prime time for blackfin. Many of the charter captains look for them around the shrimp boats. If you catch it right with a shrimp boat, the fishing can be as fast and furious as anything you've ever experienced. According to Captain Mike Delph, "I could put a blindfold on you and you would still catch a tuna on a fly."

Captain Jeff Burns, a retired Army Green Beret and Special Forces veteran, has the shrimp boat–blackfin tuna program down to a science. He leaves the dock before dawn to meet shrimp trawlers as they clear their nets after trawling all night. Once he locates the fleet with radar, he scans with binoculars at first light to see which boats have attracted birds, indicating that boats are clearing their nets and almost guaranteeing that blackfin tuna and false albacore will be feeding.

Yellowfin are far less common than blackfin in the keys, but the ones that are caught are often brutes. The current fly-rod world record for yellowfin tuna is 95 pounds 14 ounces. While landing 100-pound bluefin tuna on a fly rod no longer raises eyebrows, to date no one has landed a 100-pound yellowfin on a fly. Several of the Key West guides I spoke with were confident that it is just a matter of time before the 100-pound mark for yellowfin tuna is broken, and they predicted that it would be broken at the Key West Bar, which is just 10 miles southwest of Key West.

In winter yellowfin move into the area around the bar, and while there are usually only a few small schools, the fish run big, averaging around 150 pounds. Boats anchor on the shallow side of the bar and

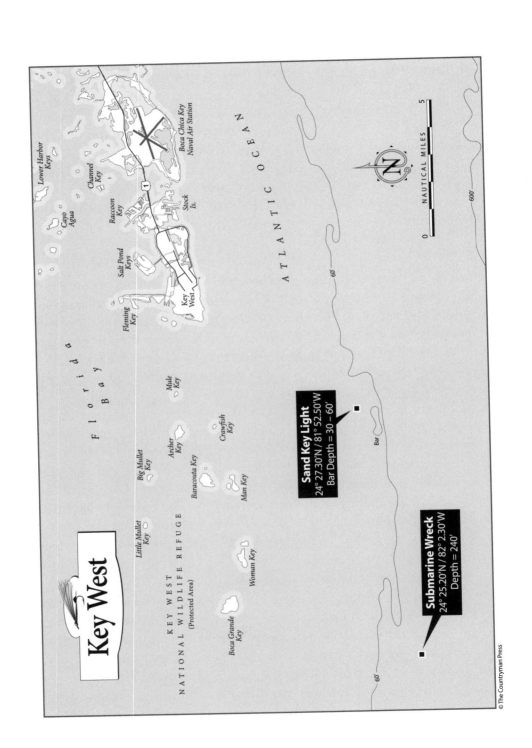

Key West

Lower Harbor Keys

Cayo Agua

Channel Key

Boca Chica Key
Naval Air Station

Raccoon Key

Stock Is.

Salt Pond Keys

Fleming Key

Key West

F l o r i d a   B a y

Little Mullet Key

KEY WEST
NATIONAL WILDLIFE REFUGE
(Protected Area)

Big Mullet Key

Archer Key

Baracouta Key

Man Key

Crawfish Key

Mule Key

Woman Key

Boca Grande Key

ATLANTIC OCEAN

60'

60'

60'

600'

Bar

Sand Key Light
24° 27.30'N / 81° 52.50'W
Bar Depth = 30 – 60'

Submarine Wreck
24° 25.20'N / 82° 2.30'W
Depth = 240'

N

0   NAUTICAL MILES   5

© The Countryman Press

chum with live pilchards to bring monster yellowfin right up to the transom. The yellowfin get so fired up chasing the live pilchards that they will readily take a fly, so getting them to eat is not the problem. It's what you do after the hookup that can be problematical.

Spice Up Your Chumming

Nothing gets my heart racing like tuna slicing through schools of terrified baitfish, churning the surface into white foam. Unfortunately, this doesn't happen as often as I would like in my pursuit of tuna. While drifting a fly back in a chum slick isn't my favorite way to target tuna, when they aren't showing I have no problem resorting to chum. And the Florida guides have really spiced up chumming.

All the Florida guides I've fished with carry large aerated live wells on their boats. They fill these with saltwater and thousands of live baits like pilchards or threadfin minnows to use as live chum. Once they get their boat over the structure they plan to fish, they start tossing out handfuls of baitfish. If tuna are around, it's usually just a matter of minutes before they are busting through live bait chum on the surface.

The artificial blitzes these guides create are amazing to watch and easier to fish, unlike the run-and-gun blitz fishing I'm used to in my

TOM GILMORE

A live well filled with pilchards

Northeast fishing, where you try to get the boat in position in front of a school of fish crashing bait on the surface. The live chum not only stay near the boat, but they also use it as structure to hide from predators. The boat is their best safe haven, and when the prey species start coming at the boat it's usually with tuna on their tails. Needless to say, it's a very exciting way to fish.

Naturals and Their Imitations

On the mainland side of the Outer Banks of North Carolina there are two of the largest bait-producing estuaries on the planet, Albemarle and Pamlico sounds. In the fall when their waters start to chill, tons of prey species start their southerly winter migration out of the sounds. At times there are millions of bay anchovy, silversides, and other prey species pouring out of the inlets past waiting predators. This is what fuels the great false albacore run off Harkers Island and provides the food chain for all the tuna in the region.

The bait that locals are looking for is menhaden, or bunker. These big, oily baits really get the big striped bass and yellowfin and bluefin tuna fired up. For menhaden patterns, a wide-profile fly would be a good choice, and no one should be surprised that the Lefty's Deceiver is the go-to fly on the Outer Banks.

If we are chunking for tuna sitting back in a chum slick and not responding to a moving fly, I'll cut off the rear half of a Deceiver just past the bend in the hook, drift it back with the real fish chunks, and hold on for dear life. To match the smaller baits, the locals favor Bob Clouser's Deep Minnow, both the traditional pattern and Tom Earnhardt's version, which is tied with translucent synthetic materials.

As I mentioned before, offshore fly fishing has very few devotees in Bermuda, so it's not surprising that they haven't developed their own regional fly patterns. In fact, one of the locals described his favorite fly as "a stainless-steel hook with some white materials and an eye on it."

Bermuda's predominant prey species include anchovies, squid, and flying fish. For squid, you could use large Deceivers or a realistic squid fly like Bob Popovics's Shady Lady Squid. When the fish are feeding on flying fish, I always go to a surface popper. Nothing beats the thrill of seeing a tuna chase down a surface popper.

If the tuna are feeding on anchovies or if that's what the crew is chumming with, I'll fish one of Popovics's Surf Candies. The anchovy pattern that performed best in the Bermuda Fly Fishing Invitational was the Gummy Minnow, which was developed by Blane Chocklett. According to Captain Keith Winter, this rubber fly is a dead ringer for an anchovy, and Blane makes both a floating and a sinking version.

In South Florida the prime bait used for live chum is the scaled sardine or pilchard. The pilchard, or greenie as the locals call them, is hardier than the herring and anchovy species in the region, and therefore lasts longer in the live well. Most of the Florida captains use small green-and-white Deceivers to match the pilchard, but I prefer a synthetic pattern developed by Captain Scott Hamilton.

The Hamilton Special is tied largely with a nylon hair that Sea Striker, Inc. makes for jigs. It's stiffer than most synthetics on the market and it doesn't foul. Scott finishes off this fly with two large 3-D epoxy eyes. He ties several thousand Hamilton Specials a year and goes to the trouble and expense of adding eyes. He contends that very often the eyes make a tremendous difference in your catch rate, and I strongly agree with him.

The Gulf of Mexico

The year 2005 was devastating for the coastal communities that line the waters of the Gulf of Mexico. The Gulf Coast states were pummeled by three major hurricanes, none more destructive than Katrina, a Category 5 hurricane that struck in late August. Katrina wreaked havoc all along the coasts of Alabama, Mississippi, and Louisiana.

Shortly after Katrina, Hurricane Rita struck the coasts of western Louisiana and Texas. In addition to the tragic impact these storms had on human life, property, and regional economies, they devastated the region's natural resources. Legendary fishing hamlets like Venice, Port Sulphur, and Shell Beach, Louisiana, which added so much to the charm and culture of the Mississippi Delta, were destroyed.

After the storms, I wondered if there would even be an attempt to rebuild these villages and if the way of life would ever be the same. I wondered what resources the charter captains would have, and I was particularly concerned about Captain Scott Avanzino, who just weeks before severe Katrina guided me to my largest fly-rod yellowfin between two smaller tropical storms.

Well, just 10 days after Katrina I got the answer I was hoping for. Somehow, not only did Scott get his boats out of harm's way, he also was able to make this posting on his Web site: "A blessing to fish today." There was a picture of Scott holding a large yellowfin tuna and smiling from ear to ear. He was back in business, and I was very impressed with his resourcefulness and that of his fellow captains.

Captain Scott Avanzino with a yellowfin caught just ten days after Hurricane Katrina

The Game in the Gulf

The name of the game in the Gulf of Mexico is to find a shrimper. From Key West to Texas, the best bluewater fly fishing is around shrimp boats. Find a shrimp boat culling through its bycatch and you'll have false albacore (called bonito or boneheads in the gulf), blackfin, and yellowfin tuna, often by the thousands. While I'm appalled by the amount of bycatch (nontarget species) associated with trawling for shrimp, it does create some wild fishing opportunities for tuna and other game species looking for a free meal. And at least the cull is going back into the water and remains part of the food chain.

False albacore have a reputation for being fly fishing's hottest fish from Cape Cod, Massachusetts, to Cape Lookout, North Carolina, but in the gulf they are considered trash fish. They are scorned for grabbing a lure or fly before a blackfin or treasured yellowfin can get to it. Some conventional-tackle charter captains who target yellowfin tuna even have disdain for blackfin tuna, a real prize for fly anglers. I know several Louisiana captains who even use false albacore and blackfin tuna for chum.

Generally the shrimp boats trawl during the night and cull their catch at first light. This creates immense chum slicks that often draw thousands of hungry predators and keep them up near the surface until the food line stops. I always try to book with guides who are in constant contact with shrimpers. The shrimpers know the water—they sometimes stay out for weeks at a time, and they "feed" tuna every morning. They will gladly share information and some fresh chum in exchange for beer, cigars, newspapers, and other supplies they need onboard.

While it is obvious that the immense chum slicks draw tuna, the consensus among charter captains from the Gulf of Maine to the Gulf of Mexico is that the tuna move in as soon as they hear a trawler's gear scraping and banging. If the trawlers aren't culling, it is often possible for anglers to toss chum into their wake from a safe distance and lure a school of predators away. Good chummers can keep a school of tuna near the boat for hours.

If no trawlers are working in the area, captains will fish structure, either natural or one of the more than four thousand man-made structures, such as the oil and gas rigs that dot the offshore waters of the Gulf of Mexico. Although yellowfin tuna are the bread-and-butter fish for the gulf charter fleets, conventional-gear anglers also land bluefin and

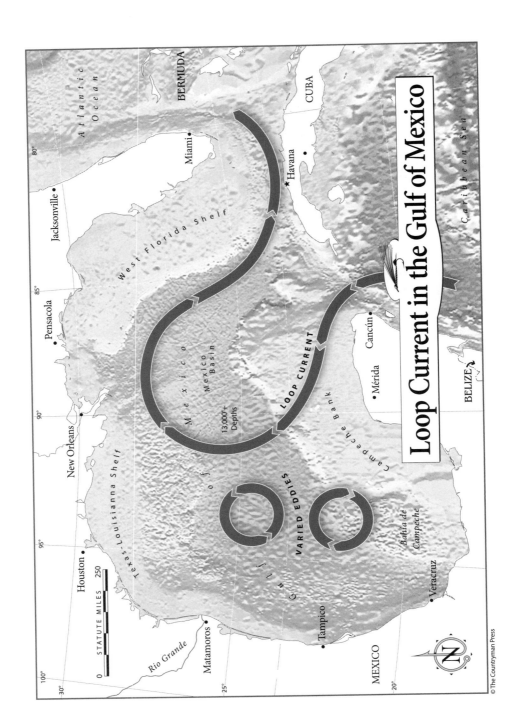

Loop Current in the Gulf of Mexico

TOM GILMORE

Bycatch from trawlers is a favorite of tuna.

bigeye tuna, and both conventional and fly anglers take blackfin, skip-jack, and false albacore. The Gulf of Mexico is one of the few areas in the world that has a large, nonmigratory blackfin population—enormous schools of blackfin can be found here year-round.

Florida Panhandle

The Loop Current is a warm current that comes up from the Caribbean and enters the Gulf of Mexico near the Yucatan Peninsula, bringing with it a richness of plankton—the base of the food chain. The loop travels northeast and comes closest to shore off Louisiana and the Florida Panhandle before heading southeast toward the Florida Keys. There it enters the Atlantic between the keys and Cuba and joins the north-flowing Gulf Stream.

As the Loop Current passes throughout the Desoto Canyon off the Florida Panhandle, it causes upwellings at famous fishing hot spots like the Spur, Nipples, and, farther offshore, the Squiggles. (These really are panhandle tuna hot spots, not gentlemens' clubs.)

These upwellings bring plankton to the surface, which attracts bait-fish and, with them, predators such as false albacore, blackfin and yellowfin tuna, and dolphin—all, by the way, favorite foods for blue and white marlin.

In many cases, eddies branch off the Loop Current and drift northwest closer to shore. When this happens it's not uncommon to find bluewater within 40 miles of Panama City or Destin Pass. Out at the 100-fathom line, the Elbow and the Dump provide hot midsummer action with the possibility of landing little tunny, blackfin, skipjacks, and yellowfin in a single outing. A good jumping-off point is Destin, a small town on the northwest coast of Florida with over 150 boats for charter.

Alabama and Mississippi

Alabama is the smallest state in terms of gulf shoreline. Offshore charters can be found in the port towns of Dauphin Island and Orange Beach. Most of these charters fish to the east in the deep bluewater off western Florida. These waters are comparatively close to shore, so Alabama charters usually fish the same waters as boats out of Pensacola and Destin, Florida.

Mississippi's Gulf Coast is only about 90 miles wide. The run to bluewater is very long from local ports, so tuna charters are rare in Mississippi. Some captains will make the run, but you would be better served fishing out of Louisiana.

Louisiana

The gulf provides good tuna fishing all along the 100-fathom line from Key West to East Texas, and this is within the range of most sport-fishing boats. But I think the best place to target tuna in the entire gulf is the waters off the Mississippi River Delta. Offshore sport-fishing in Louisiana is a fairly recent development.

The New Orleans Big Game Fishing Club got things started in the early 1960s when it hosted Big Game tournaments out of Grande Isle. Today Louisiana can boast of its tremendous blue marlin, white marlin, sailfish, dolphin, and blackfin and yellowfin tuna fisheries. Most of the bluewater charters come out of Grand Isle or Venice in the Mississippi Delta region. Venice has several captains who are fly-rod friendly and a few who actually cater to bluewater fly-rodders.

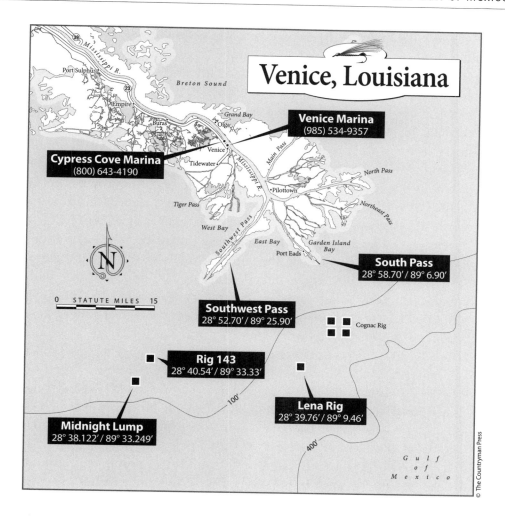

Venice

Venice sits at the mouth of the mighty Mississippi River, which is about a 90-minute drive south from New Orleans. The charter captains out of Venice proclaim it is the year-round tuna capital of the world. That is quite a claim for this tiny, remote hamlet, the last outpost on the Mississippi Delta and home to oil-rig workers, commercial fishermen, and a handful of charter captains. The town once had a sign that read, "Welcome to the end of the world."

So how does Venice stack up against some of the more legendary tuna ports on the East Coast and around the world? Well, if you're looking for a fly-rod record yellowfin tuna, Venice should be at the top of your list.

The current IGFA fly-rod record for yellowfin is 95 pounds 14 ounces, taken off Carnarvon, Australia. In Venice, landing a 100-pound-plus yellowfin tuna on conventional tackle is a daily occurrence. Captain Peace Marvel, who has pioneered much of the offshore fly fishing from Venice, told me that it's not uncommon to have dozens of 150-pound yellowfin just a few feet off the stern of the boat eating everything thrown to them. He predicts it's just a matter of time until a 100-pound yellowfin is landed on a fly.

Numerous factors make Venice one of the best tuna towns on the planet. For one thing, the surrounding waters are rich with nutrients flowing into the gulf from the Mississippi River. Sonny Eirich, CEO of Cypress Cove Marina, describes the fishery this way: "The natural-gas rigs off Louisiana's coast form the world's largest artificial reef system, and when you combine the artificial structures we have offshore with the Barataria-Terrebonne estuarine complex—the world's largest, most productive estuary system—it's easy to see that we have a fishery here unmatched and unexcelled worldwide."

The Loop Current, or rip as locals call it, often comes within 3 miles of the mouth of the Mississippi River and can generally be found no more than 20 miles out. It is quite a sight to see the muddy water of the Mississippi River being held at bay by the cobalt-blue conveyer belt of food. The rip can stretch 100 miles across the delta, and the line is often as clear and clean as if it were drawn with a pen.

It gathers everything in its path: flotsam, tons upon tons of golden sargasso weed, and, most importantly, fish. While the weather can be a problem from fall into spring, the Sackett Banks or Midnight Lump offer fly anglers the best tuna and wahoo fishing in the world. Captain Marvel has convinced me that the next fly-rod world-record yellowfin tuna will come from this area. The biggest tuna on a fly taken there to date is 74 pounds, but Marvel and his clients have hooked dozens in the 100- to 150-pound range on a fly rod; it's only a matter of time until one makes it to the boat.

While Venice has tuna year-round, there are two major runs of yellowfin. The late winter–spring run is made up mostly of tuna in the 30- to 60-pound range. They show between February and May and thin out in the summer. The gulf provides a consistent yellowfin fishery throughout the summer, but you have to venture farther offshore. Big fish of 100 to 150 pounds are more plentiful during the fall and winter, but they are still fairly common during the spring, and year-round you can fish for blackfin up to 30 pounds.

Night fishing for blackfin tuna is very productive at the rigs that are on the edge of or in the deep water off the continental shelf. Venice is the last outpost accessible by land along the Mississippi River. It is closer to bluewater than any other port along the gulf. From most ports, you'll need to go 50 miles offshore to get into 400 feet of water. Venice has 400 feet of water less than 6 miles out, 1,000 feet 10 miles out, and 3,000 feet 23 miles offshore. The two marinas in Venice, Cypress Cove and Venice, were devastated by Katrina. They are being rebuilt and will be open for business well before you read this.

Offshore Platforms

The offshore oil and gas rigs are mammoth structures capable of attracting and holding incredible quantities of bait. At night these rigs are lit up like Christmas trees, providing additional attraction for prey species and setting the table for some unparalleled night fishing.

Tuna are almost constant eaters, consuming as much as 30 to 40 percent of their body weight daily. Captain Scott Avanzino, who runs a lot of overnight tuna trips to the deepwater rigs, reports that blackfin favor squid and that yellowfin love flying fish. Both squid and flying fish become more active at night and bring tuna closer to the surface. Scott likes a thin, pink squid fly for the blackfin and surface poppers to imi-

JEFF PIERCE

Night fishing near oil rigs is very productive in the gulf.

tate flying fish for the yellowfin. Yellowfin tuna prefer deeper water than the blackfin, but any rig in 300 feet or more of water can hold yellowfin.

For serious yellowfin outings the best spot off Louisiana, if not in the whole gulf, is the Midnight Lump. On nautical charts the lump is referred to as the Sackett Bank. Because it's only 18 to 20 miles offshore, in late fall and winter when the tuna are running there could be as many as a hundred boats fishing here. The lump is a muddy hump that rises about 212 feet in water that is 420 feet deep, and the water moving over it causes an upwelling that delivers disoriented prey species to the tuna and other predators that gather for the feast. The boats anchor there and chum the tuna into casting range.

When chumming, you always want to give the tuna enough food to keep their interest but not enough to fill them up. Captain Marvel claims that with the number of tuna that gather on the lump, overfeeding would be very hard to do! How good can the lump be? Well, during the winter of 2003 Captain Marvel had 41 consecutive successful trips for yellowfin tuna. During several trips he reported seeing 150-pound tuna jumping 10 feet out of the water "skyjacking" flying fish, and on calm days he could see them busting miles away.

Cocodrie

Captain Tommy Pellegrin, who runs Custom Charters out of Cocodrie, Louisiana, targets blackfin 55 miles south of Cocodrie in 200 to 250 feet of water. Like so many of the guides in the gulf, Tommy has a good relationship with the shrimp boats, often trading beer for bycatch to set up his chum slick. Tommy was quick to point out that even if a shrimp boat isn't culling bycatch, that doesn't mean tuna aren't around. This fits with the theory so many guides subscribe to that tuna recognize the sound of nets and chains dragging the bottom and the diesel engines, so it pays to get behind a shrimper and start chumming.

You'll be surprised by the number of fish waiting for a meal. Tommy readily admits that due to its close proximity to land—18 miles off the Mississippi Delta—the Midnight Lump is the favorite spot of most yellowfin anglers. He claims there are plenty of tuna south of Houma in the Green Canyon, even more than at the lump, but the canyon is 80 miles offshore. He also fishes a lump twice the size of the Midnight Lump that is just as productive, but it's about 70 miles offshore. If you want tuna action away from the crowds and you don't mind a long boat ride, give Captain Tommy Pellegrin a call.

Texas

Ask any Texas charter captain how he finds tuna and his answer will be the same as captains throughout the gulf: Find a shrimp boat. Also consistent with other gulf captains, when there are no shrimp boats around, the Texas captains target tuna in the waters surrounding the offshore wrecks and rigs.

Most boats are after blackfin tuna, which are much more common in the Texas offshore waters than yellowfin tuna. During the summer, it's possible to have daytime surface blitzes as blackfin plow through schools of menhaden and flying fish. But most captains agree that for Texas tuna, your best option is night fishing under the lights of oil rigs. In fact, some captains will fish blackfin only at night.

While yellowfin are not as common in Texas as blackfin, sport-fishing boats find them out beyond the 100-fathom curve off Freeport and Port Aransas. Captain Charlie Stetzel, who fishes out of Freeport and has quite an impressive list of tournament records for both yellowfin tuna and blue marlin, would be my go-to guy if I wanted to target tuna in Texas.

Charlie is an avid fly fisherman with an impressive fishing resume from around the world. Although most of his clients fish conventional tackle, he welcomes fly anglers. In 2005 he had an overnight trip in which his anglers quit by 4:00 A.M., exhausted by the 65 yellowfin landed, all weighing over 100 pounds. For the final few hours, Charlie or his mate had to finish the battles for his weary crew. If you do decide to charter with Captain Charlie, plan an overnight trip. Not only do the tuna bite better at night, but it's a 105-mile run to Charlie's favorite rigs, which are in 5,000 feet of water.

Naturals and Their Imitations

Throughout the gulf the guides are unanimous in that the number-one prey species for tuna is flying fish. While I can't refute that opinion, I suspect that it's due to the amount of time flying fish spend on the surface and the fact that you can't miss tuna feeding on them. Flying fish are a guide's best friend, because not only do they bring tuna to the surface so you can find them, but they also let you target them with topwater lures and flies. You will never forget the sight of a 100-pound-plus yellowfin tuna clearing the waters while running down terrified flying fish. On calm days, a tuna's reentry splash can be seen for over a mile.

Next on the tuna menu would be squid, especially at night around the lighted offshore rigs. The lights bring the squid closer to the surface, and the tuna along with them.

The gulf guides prefer blue and white flies for flying fish and use everything from Clousers and Deceivers to surface poppers. The most effective flying-fish fly that I've come across was designed by Jeff Pierce. Jeff is the sales manager for Mustad & Son. His fly is made with Flexi-Cord body material manufactured by Wapsi Fly, Inc. It is incredibly realistic, and with dozens of successful yellowfin trips under his belt, Jeff has the results to prove it.

He ties most of his tuna flies on a saltwater circle hook of his own design. When a tuna takes a fly tied on a circle hook, it gets hooked in the corner of the mouth; the tippet never rubs against the mouth, so it doesn't get frayed. Jeff claims that a fish on a circle hook stays hooked, a real plus when battling a large tuna.

For squid patterns, the guides go to large pink or white flies. Here again they prefer basic patterns like Clousers and Deceivers. I've had good luck with some of the more realistic squid patterns like Bob Popovics's Shady Lady Squid fly and Dave Skok's Squid fly.

Part IV

Stock Assessment

World Consumption and Status

13

Demand

Tuna are one of the most economically valuable animals on the planet. Commercially, they represent an annual multibillion-dollar industry. People around the globe love to eat tuna, whether it's raw, cooked, canned, grilled, or in a salad. Nutritionists tout the benefits of the omega-3 fatty acids found in tuna and Atkins dieters love tuna for its protein. Canned tuna is convenient and relatively inexpensive and out-sells all other types of canned meat worldwide. You would be hard pressed to find a diner or a deli that doesn't have tuna salad on the menu.

Over the last half of the 20th century, demand for tuna grew faster than any other food. The Japanese have built their culinary culture around tuna. Their love for sushi and sashimi has spread across the ocean to the United States, and now sushi bars are found at many upscale restaurants. Japan and the United States combined consume more tuna than the rest of the world. Americans alone consume over 400,000 metric tons of canned tuna a year.

Mercury Is Rising

The U.S. Department of Agriculture predicts that in the year 2020 we will consume 25 percent more fish than we do today, despite concerns over increased levels of mercury in some species of fish. In March 2004, the Food and Drug Administration (FDA) and the Environmental Protection Agency (EPA) issued a joint consumer advisory about mercury

Giant bluefin tuna tend to have high mercury levels.

levels in fish and shellfish. The advisory was targeted toward women who are pregnant, women who might become pregnant, nursing mothers, and young children.

The advisory indicated that fish and shellfish are an important part of a healthy diet and suggested that these groups can eat up to 12 ounces (two average meals) a week of a variety of fish and shellfish that are low in mercury. The FDA lists canned light tuna as low in mercury. The advisory went on to point out that albacore tuna canned as white tuna had more mercury than canned light tuna, and recommended that pregnant women and young children eat only up to 6 ounces (one average meal) per week.

While mercury does occur naturally in the environment, most of the mercury in our oceans comes from coal-burning power-plant emissions that settle into the water. Mercury then works its way into and up the food chain. The smaller the fish, the less likely they are to have accumulated large amounts of mercury.

The FDA recommends against eating meals of fish that have in excess of 0.05 parts per million (ppm) of mercury. Most canned tuna marketed as light tuna is skipjack, a much smaller species of tuna than albacore, which are canned as white or solid white tuna. Tests on the smaller skipjack show an average ppm of .012, and the larger albacore show an average of 0.035 ppm.

One concern that consumer advocates have is that quite often the tuna industry substitutes yellowfin tuna for skipjack tuna in their canned light products. Yellowfin can grow to be quite large and have levels of mercury as high as albacore, but both are under the FDA limit. The advocates want the industry to label the species used in canned products so that consumers can make informed decisions.

Bluefin tuna are at the top of the food chain and therefore are likely to accumulate the most mercury. In June 2005, an 873-pound bluefin tuna was landed off the state of Delaware, shattering the old state record by several hundred pounds. It also set a record for mercury, at 2.5 ppm.

The FDA stresses that there are far too many benefits from eating tuna and other seafood to give it up altogether. According to Dr. David Acheson, the chief medical officer of the FDA's Center for Food Safety, "If you eat fish according to our guidelines, you will gain the benefits and reduce your exposure to mercury."

Status

Increased demand for tuna worldwide has dramatically increased its value and resulted in more aggressive harvesting, which in turn has caused tuna numbers to plummet. Scientists report that most species of tuna have been harvested well below their maximum sustainable yield (MSY), which is the greatest amount of a species that can be harvested without impairing its ability to continue to reproduce and sustain a viable population.

According to scientists with the International Convention for the Conservation of Atlantic Tunas (ICCAT), some species like the western population of bluefin have fallen more than 80 percent since the 1970s. One of the great challenges facing fisheries management in this century will be regulating tuna harvests to support sustainable levels of reproduction.

Bluefin Tuna Management

While a comprehensive study of harvests, stock assessment, and regulations for all tuna species is well beyond the scope of this book, I want to share just how critical and difficult responsible management is for these highly migratory, highly valuable species. I have selected the bluefin tuna for my example because it is the most critically threatened of all the tuna species.

Massachusetts Division of Fisheries personnel cite three main components for the major decline of bluefin tuna in the North Atlantic: (1) the development of a purse-seine fishery in the late 1950s; (2) the development of Japanese high-seas longline fishing, also in the late 1950s; and (3) the opening of the high-priced Japanese sushi and sashimi market in the 1970s, which created a demand for giant bluefin tuna from the western Atlantic.

In a recent interview Captain Dave Preble of Rhode Island, who has chartered fishermen for tuna for over 20 years, outlined for me the history of fishing for bluefin tuna in the northwestern Atlantic.

The Marshall Plan

Then Secretary of State George Marshall, in his commencement address to Harvard University on June 5, 1947, proposed a solution to the widespread hunger, unemployment, and housing shortages that faced Europeans in the aftermath of World War II. Under the Marshall Plan, the

United States provided aid to prevent starvation in the major war areas, help European countries rebuild devastated areas, and begin economic reconstruction.

Prior to World War II, bluefin tuna were caught on rods and reels for sport in recreational tournaments, but there was no market or commercial harvest in the northwestern Atlantic. There literally was a virgin population of bluefin ready for the taking if the markets could be developed. The Bureau of Commercial Fisheries—now the National Marine Fisheries Service (NMFS)—wanted to have bluefin harvested for canning to sell to Europe as part of the Marshall Plan.

The bureau provided enough incentives for commercial fishermen that by the early 1960s several of the Pacific purse-seiners brought their boats to the Atlantic to begin fishing for bluefin tuna in New England. At first, purse-seiners targeted schoolie bluefin; the canneries preferred them and the seiners feared that the giants would damage their gear. For about 15 years, they landed approximately 12,000 tons of schoolie bluefin tuna annually. This made it hard for sustainable numbers of fish to reach sexual maturity, and by the mid-1970s there was stock recruitment failure. (Recruitment is the number of fish that grow to a catchable size in a year.)

In the early 1970s the sushi and sashimi markets exploded in Japan. The Japanese preferred bluefin from the cold waters off New England because of their high fat content. It didn't take long for the U.S. seiners to figure out how to net the giants.

Preble did a lot of sport-fishing for giants during this time and entered several annual tuna tournaments. He reports that in 1983, there were 43 giant bluefin taken during the annual Block Island tournament. Six years later, zero giant bluefin tuna were landed in the tournament.

To this day, Preble claims to have thousands of dollars in fighting chairs and 130-pound class rods rotting in his garage, hoping for the comeback of the giant bluefin tuna and a return to the glory days of bluefin fishing. He summed it up by saying, "You couldn't have designed a better plan to devastate a species, eliminate recruitment by overfishing the smaller fish, and then hammer the few remaining breeders."

Frequent Flying Fish

It is ironic how, virtually overnight, giant bluefin tuna went from being considered trash fish by the commercial fishing industry in New England to being damn near worth their weight in gold. When the Japanese started paying tens of thousands of dollars for a single fish, it created a gold-rush mentality. Everyone with a boat was targeting bluefin. It became profitable to ship fresh tuna overnight via jet to the Japanese markets.

It's hard to fathom that pieces of raw tuna being eaten in the fancy upscale sushi bars in Tokyo were most likely from fish caught by the callused, weather-beaten hands of some third-generation commercial fisherman from Gloucester, Massachusetts, just a day or two before.

One Stock Is Better Than Two

In 1966 the International Convention for the Conservation of Atlantic Tunas (ICCAT) was formed by concerned countries to coordinate international research and management of highly migratory tunas and billfish in the North Atlantic. Since 1982, ICCAT has managed North Atlantic bluefin tuna as two separate stocks—western and eastern—separated by a management boundary at the 45-degree West meridian.

The management of two stocks was based on the assumption of separate spawning grounds and minimal movements between stocks. The theory was that the western Atlantic stock bred in the Gulf of Mexico and the eastern Atlantic stock bred in the Mediterranean. Western Atlantic bluefin numbers continued to decline, and as early as 1992 ICCAT estimated that their spawning population had declined to 20 percent of its 1975 level.

To this day, ICCAT continues to manage eastern and western Atlantic bluefin tuna stocks as separate populations. This has become highly controversial, since there is a growing body of evidence from tagging studies that indicates a greater degree of stock mixing than is assumed in the management plans. We fish on this side of the Atlantic with heavy conservation restrictions while the Europeans fish largely unrestricted, landing outrageous numbers of tuna, many of them illegally small.

We know that some bluefin ride the Gulf Stream and cross the Atlantic, but just how many is still being hotly debated.

The Science

In the fall of 2004, while chasing schoolie bluefin tuna with Captain Al Anderson out of Snug Harbor, Rhode Island, I brought up the subject of tagging. As I mentioned earlier, Al has tagged more bluefin tuna than anyone else in the world, over 4,500, and written the definitive book, *Bluefin Tuna, Yesterday, Today and Tomorrow*. Anderson mentioned that he had received an invitation to attend the IGFA Hall of Fame induction for his late friend Frank Mather III. Frank had been a marine biologist, and he and a colleague, Howard Schuck, tagged and studied the movements of bluefin tuna for almost 50 years. Mather was being inducted into the Hall of Fame and given a posthumous lifetime achievement award for his research, including tagging studies of bluefin tuna.

Mather and Schuck were the first to ever tag and recover a bluefin tuna. They tagged their fish off the island of Bimini in the Bahamas during the spring of 1952, and that fall it was landed off Nova Scotia. From the early 1950s until the late 1990s, this simple tagging was the only method of tracking bluefin migrations.

While the information was useful, it had two major drawbacks. First, it revealed nothing about the fish's migration except the end point, and then only when it was captured. Second, and probably more important, this method required voluntary reporting. Anglers fishing in the eastern Atlantic are reluctant to provide information that might aid in proving a greater degree of stock mixing for fear of greater restrictions being imposed on their harvests.

Coincidentally, my good friend and colleague Dick Turner and I used to share war stories about fishing for stripers on Martha's Vineyard. I remembered Dick telling me about the monster bass he took from his uncle's boat off Gay Head. He had mentioned that his uncle was a marine biologist who worked out of Woods Hole, Massachusetts. I later discovered that not only was Frank Mather his uncle, but also that Dick would be accepting the IGFA award on his behalf.

Two of the leading modern pioneers in bluefin tagging are Dr. Molly Lutcavage, formerly with the New England Aquarium and now with the University of New Hampshire, and Dr. Barbara Block of the Monterey Bay Aquarium in California. These scientists have been tagging thousands of bluefin tuna since 1985. At first the tags provided the same information as Mather's, including the number of days at sea, length and weight when caught, and point of recovery. They also had to rely on voluntary reporting, occasionally with monetary incentives for fishermen.

Starting in 1997, these researchers began using two types of electronic tags: popup satellite tags and implantable archival tags. Dr. Lutcavage, working in collaboration with commercial and recreational fishermen, has been placing pop-up satellite tags in giant bluefin tuna in New England and Canada. She and her research team targeted spawning-sized fish and programmed their tags to detach from the fish over their presumed spawning period—April to July.

These pop-up tags don't have to rely on fishermen reporting their catch. They are programmed to transmit the stored data to satellites, which in turn forward the data to the scientists' computers. Each year,

TOM GILMORE

A small, tagged bluefin tuna being measured

about 30 percent of the tags have been reported east of the 45-degree West dividing line used in the management plan under the two-stock theory.

Dr. Block, one of the foremost tuna research experts in the world, and a team of scientists have been tagging bluefin tuna off the coast of North Carolina for almost a decade in cooperation with local fishermen. This collaboration has been a boon to the researchers and the local recreational fishing industry. The research is getting tremendous support from the local fishermen, who provide their knowledge, boats, and labor.

Until the last few years the fishing season for bluefin off the coast of North Carolina was closed before the winter run of tuna arrived. This was because the annual harvest quota would have already been landed by anglers in the Northeast. (In the last few years this hasn't been so, and the North Carolina fishermen have been able to keep some fish.) But Dr. Block and her research team were allowed to land, tag, and release bluefin. You can imagine how popular her tagging efforts were as the local captains who got the opportunity to charter a group of anglers who would fish, tag, and release as part of the research project.

This is a win-win situation, and it hopefully bodes well in the long term for bluefin tuna, since Dr. Block and her colleagues are able to more closely monitor the movements of tuna.

It is important for the U.S. commercial and recreational fishing industries to disprove the two-stock theory from which ICCAT makes all its management decisions. European scientists are currently under tremendous political pressure to come up with enough evidence to support the two-stock theory to keep the United States out of fisheries management issues in the Mediterranean. This dilemma explains why increasing numbers of commercial and recreational anglers are supporting the independent research being conducted in the United States on the movement of bluefin tuna.

Historically, ICCAT found that the western stock has been in serious decline while the eastern Atlantic stock seemed healthy. Therefore, no quota was imposed on the eastern Atlantic fishermen until 2002. The harvest of bluefin was set at 35,000 metric tons for the European community. In contrast, the western Atlantic (North American) totals at that time were just 2,500 metric tons. To make matters worse, it is widely known that many European countries underreport their catch, if they report it at all. Several countries, such as Turkey, Greece, and Italy, don't even belong to ICCAT and aren't required to report any of their bluefin tuna landings.

At its November 21, 2004, meeting in New Orleans, ICCAT rejected a proposal to further study the patterns of bluefin populations, citing lack of funds. U.S. scientists, anglers, and conservationists who back such studies charge that European government officials fear that if stronger links are established between bluefin tuna populations on the two sides of the Atlantic, there will be greater pressure to restrict harvests in Europe. Current ICCAT regulations allow an annual quota in the eastern Atlantic of 32,000 tons, but officials acknowledge that the actual catch most likely exceeds 40,000 tons. The current annual quota in the western Atlantic is just 2,055 metric tons.

In the spring of 2005, Dr. Block and a team of scientists from Stanford University released a landmark study that provides invaluable information for the framing of future management plans for this species. The study tracks the movement of hundreds of bluefin tuna, documenting where they feed and breed, and calls for stronger protective measures.

Their study, which was published in the April 28, 2005, issue of the science journal *Nature,* seems to confirm what U.S. anglers have been saying for years: that tuna from the East Coast (western Atlantic), where fishing regulations are strict and quotas are low, are crossing the ocean to areas where quotas are high and regulations are often ignored. The recovery of tagged tuna demonstrates that with this high degree of mixing, the two stocks of tuna should be managed as one.

The study also indicates that some adolescent tuna from the east feed in the western Atlantic until they are old enough to breed, at which point they go back to the Mediterranean spawning grounds. Dr. Block's report, as well as studies by Dr. Lutcavage, shows that giant bluefin tuna regularly forage in the central Atlantic. The scientists called for stronger protective measures in the northern Atlantic foraging areas as well as in their breeding areas.

According to Dr. Block, we can't conserve the western Atlantic populations without protecting these fish in the central Atlantic. Eastern high-seas long-liners are impacting the recovery of western bluefin tuna. The study also raises the issue of longline bycatch in the Gulf of Mexico. While no harvest of bluefin tuna is allowed in the Gulf of Mexico, longline boats fishing for yellowfin and other species are killing significant numbers of bluefin tuna on their breeding grounds.

The scientists called for regulators to rethink how they set tuna quotas and to acknowledge that tuna hatched on both sides of the Atlantic are intermingling. They urged ICCAT to consider closing fisheries and called on the federal government to close parts of the Gulf of Mexico to longline boats when bluefin are breeding there.

The evolution of electronic tags will give us the science to monitor and regulate tuna worldwide—but not the political will to do so. If the eastern Atlantic countries refuse to cut back on their harvests, stronger restrictions and conservation measures in the western Atlantic will be for naught, and the bluefin tuna in our waters may suffer the same fate as the once-plentiful buffalo and passenger pigeon, which were hunted to extinction in an alarmingly short time span.

Fishing Regulations

14

Recreational Fishing

The first large recreationally caught bluefin tuna was taken in 1898 by Charles F. Holder off the coast of Catalina Island in California. His rod-and-reel catch weighed 183 pounds, quite remarkable when you consider that he was fishing alone in a rowboat. He fought the fish for close to four hours using a reel that didn't even have a drag. Word of the unprecedented catch spread quickly and launched the big-game sport-fishing craze in Southern California, spawning the formation of tuna clubs all along the West Coast.

In 1915 a fish caught in the North Atlantic broke the world record for bluefin. Subsequently New England's recreational fishermen began forming tuna clubs, and charter captains started to target giant bluefin tuna. In 1924 famous writer Zane Grey landed a then western Atlantic world-record bluefin weighing 758 pounds. Author Ernest Hemingway also took his share of giants.

The Sharp Cup in Nova Scotia was one of several distinguished international fishing tournaments. It was held from the early 1930s until the 1960s, with a peak landing of 1,760 bluefin in 1949.

In the early 1960s the numbers of bluefin landed began to shrink due to population decline caused by overharvesting and the lack of regulations, and late in that decade the prestigious Sharp Cup tournament was forced to cancel due to the lack of bluefin tuna.

Today giant bluefin tuna numbers in New England are so low that both recreational and commercial anglers are unable to harvest their

199

quotas. The last four years of fishing for giants in New England have been the worst in history. However, there is some hope for the future of this fishery, since scientists feel that 1994–1997 were good year classes for reproduction. Western bluefin tuna reach sexual maturity at about 7 to 11 years of age, which helps explain the dramatic increase in the number of schoolie bluefin reported in recent years in New England and the Mid-Atlantic states.

The increasing number of small bluefin tuna has really fueled the explosion of interest in fly fishing for tuna. There has also been a fairly recent discovery of the wintering population of medium and giant bluefin tuna off Cape Hatteras south to Morehead City, North Carolina, a welcome boost to the economy of several coastal communities.

After the severe decline of bluefin tuna, charter captains from the Mid-Atlantic region south to the Gulf of Mexico were forced to focus more on yellowfin tuna. Yellowfin are found in warmer waters than bluefin and don't venture into our nearshore waters, so to target them boats need to run out to the Gulf Stream or deepwater offshore canyons. As boat manufacturers improved speed and efficiency, more and more captains were willing to make the long runs to the offshore waters for yellowfin.

Because yellowfin grow quickly and reach sexual maturity in two years or less, they seem to have maintained stable populations despite the increased fishing pressure. It is common for charters fishing off North Carolina's Outer Banks and in the Gulf of Mexico to take their daily limit, which currently is three yellowfin per angler, per day.

A substantial party boat–charter boat fishery now exists for tuna, with thousands of recreational anglers targeting them from the Gulf of Maine to the Gulf of Mexico. While the sale of tuna is not allowed from charter boats, the fishery still contributes significantly to the economies of many coastal towns. It brings business to the local motels, restaurants, marinas, tackle shops, and gas stations. Charter boats for recreational fishing are known as the "six-pack" fleet, since Coast Guard licenses limit them to six passengers and two crew members.

The late Stephen Sloan, author of *Ocean Bankruptcy: World Fisheries on the Brink of Disaster*, wrote, "The economics of sport fishing are as great a value as the commercial landings of 49 states. Alaska is the exception, because its landings of commercial fish products are as large as the other 49 combined." The U.S. Commerce Department's National Oceanic and Atmospheric Administration (NOAA) reports

GENE QUIGLEY

Bluefin anglers help support a strong recreational economy.

that marine recreational fishing supports nearly 350,000 jobs and generates $30 billion annually in economic impact in the nation.

In addition, some states like Louisiana generate additional revenues through recreational fishing license fees. According to published reports from the National Marine Fisheries Service, there are over 10 million recreational anglers in the United States, and while they account for only 3 percent of finfish landings, they spend over $21 billion dollars annually. Commercial fishing accounts for 97 percent of the landings but spends only $1.6 billion a year.

The bottom line is that when developing fishing regulations the NMFS should place its highest priority on protecting species and recognize that it makes sound economic sense to protect the recreational fishing industry.

Management Authority

Atlantic tunas are managed under the dual authority of the Magnuson-Stevens Fishery Conservation and Management Act and the Atlantic Tunas Convention Act (ATCA). The latter authorizes the U.S. Secretary of Commerce to implement the binding recommendations of the International Commission for the Conservation of Atlantic Tunas (ICCAT).

The Department of Commerce has delegated the authority to manage the U.S. Atlantic tuna fisheries to the National Marine Fisheries Service, Highly Migratory Species Management Division. NMFS is a division of NOAA, which in turn is a division of the federal Department of Commerce. In April 1999, NMFS adopted its current plan for managing Atlantic tunas.

Eight tuna species occur in the western Atlantic, and five are regulated: bluefin, yellowfin, skipjack, albacore, and bigeye. The take of little tunny (false albacore), bonito, and blackfin is unrestricted. All boat owners who plan to fish for a regulated species must obtain one of two permits. The first is an Atlantic tunas permit, which is issued in five commercial categories: general, harpoon, purse seine, longline, and trap. The other is an Atlantic highly migratory species (HMS) vessel permit, which is issued in two categories: recreational angling and charter/headboat.

Only tuna taken on vessels permitted in one of the commercial categories may sell tuna. Obtaining the appropriate permit is simple; go online at www.nmfspermits.com or call 1-888-872-8862. Approximately 30,000 permits are issued each year to vessels that fish for tuna.

Limits

Currently there are no limits on the number of bigeye, albacore, yellowfin, and skipjack tunas that may be landed by a commercial vessel with an Atlantic tunas permit, and no permit is required to commercially fish for blackfin, bonito, and false albacore. Recreational anglers are limited to three yellowfin tuna per person per day, and there is no limit, with the exception of bluefin, on the number of other species of tuna that can be taken by recreational anglers.

There is a minimum size for bluefin, yellowfin, and bigeye of 27 inches curved fork length (CFL). This is the sole criterion for determining the size class of Atlantic tunas. Measurements must be taken in a straight line, tracing the contour of the body from the tip of the upper jaw to the fork of the tail.

Due to the devastation of bluefin stocks over the past few decades, they are the most highly regulated tuna species. The restrictions on the number that can be taken are complex. They vary by the category of permit you fish with and the size of fish you land, and they also change seasonally. I strongly recommend that you check the NMFS Web site at www.nmfspermits.com or call 1-888-872-8862 to confirm the current size and retention limits.

Size-Class Categories for Bluefin Tuna

Size Class	Curved Fork Length	Approximate Weight
Young School	<27"	<14 lbs.
School	27" – <47"	14 – <66 lbs.
Large School	47" – <59"	66 – <135 lbs.
Small Medium	59" – <73"	135 – <235 lbs.
Large Medium	73" – <81"	235 – <310 lbs.
Giant	81" or >	310 lbs. or >

Quotas

Only bluefin tuna are subject to an annual quota, which is allocated by the various categories of permits. For the bluefin fishing year of 2005 (June 1, 2005–May 31, 2006) the quota for all U.S.–permitted vessels is 2,055 metric tons. National Marine Fisheries Service sets aside a reserve of 45.9 metric tons to be used for in-season adjustments and independent research.

The metric ton (mt) quotas by permit category are as follows: general, 908.3; purse seine, 530.0; longline, 188.4; harpoon, 90.0; angling, 288.6; and trap, 3.8. For the 2005–2006 season, the general category closed having landed only 233.7mt out of its adjusted total of 708.3mt quota. Due to the unprecedented number of metric tons remaining in the general category during the fishing season, NMFS transferred 200 metric tons to a reserve category, which would allow the agency to account for potential overharvests in other categories. But none of the other categories came close to harvesting their quotas.

The harpoon category closed its season landing 23.1mt out of its 90mt quota, and the purse-seine category closed its season landing only 178.3mt out of its 530mt allocation. This again underscores the dangerous condition of the western Atlantic bluefin tuna population.

Permit Categories

General

The general category is for commercial fishing with hand gear, including rod and reel, hand line, and harpoon. These methods of harvest have very little negative impact on marine habitat and nontargeted fish and other marine life. Fishermen in this category are allocated, and land, the most tonnage of bluefin tuna. They are permitted to fish for giants and large mediums but are prohibited from targeting school and small-medium bluefin tuna that have not yet reached spawning age.

Harpoon

Harpoon, or stick, boats represent one of the oldest, resource-protective ways of harvesting fish. Harpooning is still practiced today, especially off the coasts of Massachusetts, Rhode Island, and the Outer Banks of North Carolina. Harpoon boats are built with a tall crow's nest for spotting fish and long bow "pulpits" or walkways to get the "stickman" close enough for a shot at the fish before the boat spooks it.

Harpooning, or sticking, is the most difficult and challenging method of fishing. Being a good stickman takes great skill and nerves of steel. As in a last-second field goal in football, the pressure is always on the stickman. A crew's livelihood rests on its stickman being good in the clutch. Harpoon boats can fish in the harpoon and general permit categories.

Purse Seine

The first commercial purse seine boat, the F/V *Silver Mink,* arrived in the western Atlantic in the late 1950s and was followed by a second in the early 1960s. Today there are only five purse-seine vessels with permits to fish inside the 200-mile limit of the East Coast. The *Connie Jean, AA Ferrante, Eileen Marie, White Dove,* and *Ruth-Pat* are grandfathered in the fishery, and no new purse-seine boats can obtain a permit.

With new state-of-the-art technology and the help of spotter planes, today's purse-seine boats are extremely efficient—perhaps too efficient—in the harvesting of tuna. These vessels are very large and they use smaller boats to pull giant nets around entire schools of fish. (They got the name "purse" because when the nets are drawn in, they close like a purse.)

NMFS calls the purse-seine fishery a "clean" fishery. Although the purse-seine fishery is deadly on target species, NMFS feels that there is usually very little bycatch. Several charter captains I interviewed strongly disagree with this position, pointing out that in addition to bycatch, the purse-seiners often take undersized fish.

Longline

Longline vessels are permitted to target many species of fish, including blackfin, longfin, yellowfin, and bigeye tuna. They aren't allowed to target bluefin tuna, but they are issued permits for incidental catches. This allows commercial longliners fishing for other species to land a limited number of bluefin. Their quota for 2005 was 188.4 metric tons of bycatch of protected species. These vessels set lines, sometimes as long as 100 miles, containing thousands of baited hooks.

Trap

Very few permits are issued in the trap category, and they're for incidental take of bluefin tuna. Currently, the trap category is allocated 0.1 percent of the total commercial landings.

Angling

The HMS angling category is for recreational rod and reel. Recreational anglers are allowed to keep, but not sell, a very limited number of bluefin tuna. The size and seasons vary greatly, so it's a good idea for recreational anglers to check the NMFS Web site for current information. Recreational anglers, including the captain and mate, can keep three yellowfin tuna per angler, per day. Yellowfin and bigeye tuna must be at least 27 inches CFL to keep, but there is no limit on the number of bigeye or any other species of tuna that recreational anglers may keep.

Charter/Headboat

As I mentioned earlier, bluefin tuna regulations are complex. One reads, "Persons aboard a vessel issued a HMS charter/headboat permit may retain and land bluefin tuna under the daily limits and quotas applicable to the angling category or the general category. The size of the first bluefin retained on an HMS charter/headboat will determine the fishing category applicable to the vessel that day."

This means that anglers could be fishing under commercial regulations (general) or recreational regulations (angling) depending on the size of the first fish they keep. Again, it's a good idea to check the current regulations before targeting tuna.

Conservation 15

The goal of fisheries management is to support a sustainable yield, which requires not harvesting at a rate greater than the species can reproduce to sustain its population. For highly migratory species like tuna, establishing what constitutes a sustainable yield is exceptionally difficult. First, you have the nearly impossible task of defining the current stock assessments. Then you must factor in different harvesting methods, supply of prey species, varying scientific theories, domestic and international political issues, and different cultures, traditions, and economics.

Issues of illegal, unreported, and unregulated fisheries add to the daunting task of fisheries management. While there are no easy answers, there are a few steps we could take that would have an immediate, positive impact on fish stocks.

Eliminate Longline Fishing

First and foremost would be the complete elimination of longline fishing. A longline vessel can have fishing lines close to 100 miles long and armed with thousands of hooks. The industry places about 750 million hooks in our oceans annually. They indiscriminately take protected fish and other sea life, including endangered seabirds and turtles, most of which die. Some pelagic longliners discard 40 to 65 percent of their harvest as bycatch, but those figures are suspiciously low, since that is just what the industry reports. It is estimated that their annual bycatch of sharks alone is 8.3 million animals.

U.S. resource managers turn their backs on the fact that the longline industry is illegally killing endangered species of birds, fish, and turtles. The commercially valuable and legal-sized fish are kept, but millions of tons of marine life are wasted annually, including small tuna that will never be able to reproduce. This is a terrible waste of the public's resources. Fortunately, some areas are off-limits to longline fishing in order to protect federally endangered species like leatherback and loggerhead turtles.

In June 2005, the Monterey Bay Aquarium and four other conservation organizations petitioned the National Marine Fisheries Service to ban all longline fishing in the Gulf of Mexico when and where western Atlantic bluefin tuna spawn. The call for the proposed ban comes after a recent study showed that under current regulations many bluefin tuna are caught and killed accidentally on their spawning grounds.

The proposed ban would last about three months, from April through June, and cover about 125,000 square miles of the northern Gulf of Mexico. Although no intentional longline fishing for bluefin is allowed in the gulf, longline boats targeting yellowfin inadvertently catch bluefin. So far, no ban has been instituted.

While most scientists agree that protecting spawning bluefin in the gulf won't solve the whole problem, it's definitely a good start. Representatives for the U.S. commercial fishing industry, not surprisingly, don't support the closing of longline fishing in the Gulf of Mexico during the bluefin breeding season. The one thing that they and the scientists do agree on is the need to tighten regulations in the Mediterranean, where young bluefin are caught and raised in cages, as well as in the central Atlantic, which is heavily fished by Japan.

It was heartening for me to learn recently that Taiwan was stepping up and starting to initiate measures to reduce the harvest of bigeye tuna. Taiwan is one of the top tuna-catching nations in the world, and in response to a United Nations call to protect bigeye tuna stocks and related resources, Taiwan agreed to dismantle 75 longline tuna boats in 2005. They plan to dismantle another 47 boats in 2006, thereby reducing their fleet by 20 percent, from 614 to 492.

While this is still a staggering number of longline vessels, Taiwan took a significant step, especially when you consider that it was voluntary and that they're not even a member of the United Nations. Their government has also agreed to spend a total of $121 million to compensate for losses suffered by the boat operators.

Protect Prey Species

Prey species such as Atlantic menhaden (*Brevoortia tyrannus*), also known as bunker or porgy, are one of the most important creatures that swim in our oceans. Commercial interests have targeted them for over a century. They are sold as bait, cattle feed, and fertilizer, and their oils are used in paints and cosmetics.

Menhaden are targeted in some areas with the use of spotter planes and purse-seine boats. Many Atlantic coastal states have eliminated menhaden harvests, but other states such as Virginia still have substantial harvests. Except for a recent quota in the Chesapeake Bay, the 15-state Atlantic States Marine Fisheries Commission (ASMFC) doesn't limit the take of menhaden, even though a decline in stock numbers is cited in ASMFC's own data.

Tuna consume as much as 40 percent of their body weight daily, so for anglers the golden rule is simple: no food, no tuna. Recreational and commercial fishermen in the Gulf of Maine report catching fewer and thinner giant bluefin tuna. In Portland, Maine, anglers report seeing truckloads of herring hauled from the docks to be sold for fertilizer and animal food. Millions of pounds of prey species are being taken out of our waters, frozen, and shipped as feed for fish farms in the eastern Atlantic and Mediterranean Sea.

Dr. Molly Lutcavage, director of the Large Pelagics Research Lab at the University of New Hampshire, has been reviewing records of landings, which confirm what New England fishermen have been reporting. Dr. Lutcavage's research is largely based on the records of Bob Campbell, manager of the Yankee Fisherman's Cooperative in Seabrook, New Hampshire. Between 1991 and 2004, Campbell's records show that over the years not only are there fewer giant bluefins being landed in the Northeast, but they are much thinner and have lower oil content. Campbell believes that a decrease in the number of herring, a staple in the bluefin diet, is a key factor.

In the Northeast, spotter plane pilots report seeing fewer bluefin tuna schools in the Gulf of Maine and also fewer whales, due largely, they feel, to the lack of prey species. The New England Fishery Management Council is now considering a more restrictive Herring Management Plan Amendment.

Campbell reports that bluefin being caught in Canada, where herring are still plentiful, remain fat and oily. A decade ago, pair trawling almost wiped out the herring population in Canadian waters. Since Canada banned both pair trawling for prey species and purse-seining for bluefin tuna, their giant bluefin fishery has recovered significantly.

Outlaw Farming

One of the major causes of the recent accelerated decline of bluefin tuna is a practice known as tuna farming. The farming of tuna, particularly bluefin, is exploding worldwide, especially in the Mediterranean. The fish targeted for farming are young, so they never get the chance to spawn. They are taken with purse-seine boats and placed in enormous pens to fatten. It takes tons of forage fish to fatten these tuna, some of which come from our waters in the western Atlantic.

Similar to salmon farms, tuna farms create a lot of waste in a concentrated area. Waste from feed and the fish themselves pollutes the surrounding waters. Also, there is the potential for large numbers of fish to be killed during storms. To make matters worse, these fish farmers have found a huge loophole in the regulations for reporting landings. Purse-seine boats never technically "land" the fish, so they don't report their catch when transferring the fish to tuna farms. Once secured in pens to be fattened, the tuna are classified as aquaculture products rather than wild fish. Therefore, amazingly, their harvest is not counted against the ICCAT quota.

Tuna farming is certainly not the answer for conservation—it is in effect purse-seining with a much more severe environmental impact.

Support Clean Harvest Methods

Increased consumer demand has greatly impacted tuna populations, especially bluefin. In the interest of conservation, I recommend that informed consumers purchase seafood for consumption that has minimal environmental impact, factoring in the relative abundance of a species and the manner in which it has been harvested.

Hand-harvest methods like rod and reel or harpooning are the only methods of taking tuna that consumers should support. These methods don't destroy habitat, and they don't kill nontarget fish and other marine life. Species like yellowfin and longfin albacore tuna mature early and are prolific reproducers, which helps them withstand fishing pressure. I encourage consumers to purchase yellowfin and albacore tuna that are caught on rod and reel, not longlines. To help guide your purchases, you can obtain a copy of the Seafood Watch Card published by the Monterey Bay Aquarium in California (www.mbayaq.org).

Recreational Anglers Should Practice Catch and Release

Whether it's due to respect for the fishery or bag limits and size restrictions, more and more anglers are practicing catch and release, and large numbers of small tuna are being released. The question is, Do they survive? The guides I interviewed were all over the map on this question. Opinions varied from high percentages of survival to a few guides reporting that they don't release any legal tuna for fear they will die and be wasted. These guides fish for tuna until their clients have the daily limit. They then require their clients to fish for other species rather than catch and release tuna and risk killing them.

Greg Skomal, a scientist with the Massachusetts Division of Marine Fisheries, has been studying catch-and-release survival rates for bluefin tuna in New England for a number of years, and his results are very encouraging. By studying a bluefin's blood chemistry, Greg is able to quantify its level of health.

His studies indicate that if there is not a lot of physical trauma inflicted by multiple hooks in a fish's mouth, dropping the fish on the deck, or having the fish out of the water too long, the likelihood of survival is actually quite good. He reports that fish that fought for 25 to 45 minutes, if properly handled, usually recover fully in one to two hours. He claims that tuna have a remarkable ability to quickly rebuild their oxygen supplies and to clean their muscles of lactic acid buildup during the strain of the fight.

Skomal also tracks released tuna using telemetry. He reports that for the first hour or so after they are released, bluefin tuna are generally very lethargic, but during the second hour their behavior reverts back to their normal movements in the water column.

He even studied the impact of bait-fishing with traditional J hooks and the newer circle hooks. His results prove that circle hooks cause much fewer injuries than J hooks. Fly fishers are just starting to experiment with flies tied on circle hooks. Jeffrey Pierce, sales manager for hook manufacturer Mustad & Son, has introduced a circle hook that he created for fly fishing. The hook is listed as their saltwater streamer hook (C71S SS).

He designed the hook with a wide enough gap that an angler can still set the hook with a strip strike. He has been fishing with circle streamer hooks for seven or eight years and his results are impressive. He reports that his worst-case scenario is missing about 15 percent of strikes, but at the end of the day he lands 95 percent of the fish hooked.

Jeff frequently fishes with Captain Peace Marvel out of Venice, Louisiana, on the Gulf of Mexico for large yellowfin tuna. He boasts that the best thing about the saltwater streamer hook is, "When you stick a big tuna, it stays stuck." I know from experience that after a long, grueling battle with a large tuna, there is nothing more demoralizing than to have the fish come "unbuttoned" beside the boat. I know I'll be testing circle hooks in the seasons ahead—they seem to hold promise for landing more fish and increasing survival rates for released fish.

New Jersey native Captain Gene Quigley reports that another advantage of using circle hooks is that they hook fish in the corner of the mouth; therefore the tippet isn't rubbing across the fish's mouth during the fight. Because of this, you can eliminate a shock tippet and one additional knot from your leader system. This saves time in rigging, and there's one less knot to fail.

Tuna are negatively buoyant. If they lie motionless, they will sink. Therefore they can never rest and must continuously swim forward. Their survival is literally based on a sink-or-swim proposition. The traditional method of reviving an exhausted fish by holding it upright and moving it back and forth in the water will kill a tuna. By design, tuna must move forward to pass water over their gills to fill them with oxygen. The best way to release a tuna is to toss it back into the water headfirst on a 45-degree angle. This will flush the gills with oxygen and jump-start its recovery.

One of the biggest threats to the survival of a released tuna, and one of my pet peeves, is photographing the fish. Don't get me wrong; the walls of my den are filled with hero shots. But I can guarantee that if you take photos of a fish you're going to release, it will diminish its chance of survival. To take quality photos and minimize the amount of time the fish is out of the water, you need to prepare ahead. The designated photographer should have the camera ready and the shot planned before the fish is landed.

How many times have we seen others—or been guilty of it ourselves—land a fish and then decide to take a photo. If you have to waste valuable time hunting through a gear bag, handing your camera to a partner, and then instructing him on how to use it, I urge you not to take the photo. Under these circumstances, you're most likely going to be disappointed with your photo, and even worse, you'll have put the survival of the fish at a much greater risk.

Plan the photos you want in advance, and instruct your fishing partner on how to use your camera before you begin fishing. Store all cameras in a dry, accessible location. Some charter captains say it's bad luck to mention wanting a photo until the fish is actually in the boat. I'm just as superstitious as the next guy, but trust me, you will land just as many fish, get better photos, and release healthier fish if you discuss picture-taking beforehand with your partners. Identify the positions you want the photographer in when the fish is landed, taking into consideration the location of the sun and the background.

If you're fishing with a guide, he'll usually land and unhook the fish. I recommend that you let your guide continue to hold the fish, so all you have to do is slide into the photo while holding your fly rod. It's quick, and there is less chance of dropping the fish. As soon as the photo is taken, the guide can quickly release the fish.

Make Sound Economic Decisions

When tuna stocks rebound—and hopefully they will—I advocate that regulators consider giving recreational anglers a bigger allocation of the fishery. Historically there have been many instances when the recreation quota has been reached or changed before the season has ended. Sudden forced closures in the recreational fishery impact not only the charter-boat owners but also the local economies, with cancellations of motel reservations and lost food, gas, and tackle sales. I have seen this happen in the Northeast on many occasions and for quite a number of years in North Carolina.

I also suggest reexamining the politics and policy of grandfathering five purse-seine boats, whose owners get rich on a public resource at the expense of everyone else. If we are going to allow them to continue to harvest tuna in this manner, they should be charged a legitimate permit fee. Those funds could then be earmarked for additional tuna research. It is absurd that purse-seine vessels pay the same $22 fee for a permit that a recreational angler does. Their quota of bluefin tuna is over 500 metric tons. For the privilege of earning millions of dollars, the five purse-seine vessels pay a total of $110 in permit fees.

Carl Safina, in his compelling book *Song for the Blue Ocean,* frames the issue succinctly when he writes, "The New England tuna netters' annual season starts in late August, and in two months each of the five seining vessels, crewed by about six or eight fishermen, will catch a million dollars worth of bluefins, their annual free allocation of a public resource, courtesy of the U.S. government."

He goes on to say, "While thousands of other fishermen struggle to earn a living from this depleted resource, these five boats provide only 3 percent of the employment in the fishery and are disproportionately allocated roughly 25 percent of the quota—and their fatly paid lobbyists work like sled dogs to ensure that they hang onto it."

Fund Tuna Research

For this highly migratory species to survive long-term, management plans will have to be built on sound science. The better the science, the better the chance we have of overcoming the political and economic obstacles that face fisheries management personnel. It is encouraging to see greater numbers of recreational and commercial fishermen working cooperatively with independent scientists to evaluate stock assessment, health, and migratory patterns.

To date, tagging studies have given us good data on where larger bluefin summer, winter over, and breed. In the last several years we have enjoyed great inshore fishing for schoolie bluefin in the Mid-Atlantic and the Northeast. The question is, Will they continue to bless our waters in the years to come, and will they live to someday become giants? Unfortunately, we have very little data on where the massive schools of schoolie bluefin come from and where they go when they leave our waters in the fall. Several charter captains I interviewed believe that these fish cross the ocean and become part of the massacre in the Mediterranean.

Hopefully, our speculation on school-sized bluefin may soon be over, thanks to a new study launched in June 2005 by the Large Pelagics Research Lab of the University of New Hampshire in cooperation with researchers from the Virginia Institute of Marine Science and the Massachusetts Division of Marine Fisheries. The program is called Tag a Tiny. Its goal is to track the movements of juvenile bluefin tuna by placing archival tags on them.

Manage Bluefin as One Stock

ICCAT must acknowledge that there is a greater degree of mixing of bluefin stocks than previously thought and revise its management to reflect current science. This would result in an international effort to set greater restrictions on harvests in the eastern Atlantic, and hopefully, when stocks start to rebound, fishermen in the western Atlantic would be allocated a fairer share of the quotas.

Tighter Controls and Enforcement in the Eastern Atlantic

Not only is the eastern Atlantic fishery allocated a quota 12 times that of the western quota, but also, according to Steve Sloan, as much as 50 percent of the bluefin harvest in the Mediterranean is fish less than 5 pounds, and many fish are less than 1 pound, which is an outrageous waste of a public resource. Many scientists and conservationists feel that once bluefin tuna pass through the Straits of Gibraltar, they are doomed. In the western Atlantic we have five purse-seine boats fishing for bluefin, but in the Mediterranean there are over five hundred boats, some with nets as large as the Minneapolis Metrodome.

According to both Sloan and Safina, reporting of landings and enforcement of quotas is not happening in much of the eastern Atlantic. Countries that do report often underreport, and many don't report at all. The leading tuna-harvesting countries must work together and demand tighter controls, reporting, and enforcement of quotas in that region. The United States and other nations must be willing to impose economic sanctions if we are going to save this spectacular species.

Final Thoughts

Fly fishing for trout has a long and hallowed history and a rich tradition dating back several centuries. Preston Jennings, in *A Book of Trout Flies*, writes that the origins of entomology and imitation are "as ancient as the rivers of third-century Macedonia." Dame Juliana Berners's work, *Treatyse of Fysshynge wyth an Angle*, which included 12 fly patterns that were an effort to "match the hatch," was written some seven centuries ago.

The fascination with match-the-hatch fly fishing in North America dates back to the mid-1800s. Austin Francis, in *Catskill Rivers*, details the history of trout fishing in the Northeast. He writes, "Transportation played a major role in developing American fly fishing. The biggest role in opening up the trouting regions and introducing the masses to the sport was played by the railroads. They carried fishermen to the region and provided transportation for the trout hatcheries." Between 1851 and 1872 the railroads cut through the Catskill and Pocono mountains, giving city-dwelling anglers access to pristine rivers and streams with abundant trout populations.

Saltwater fly fishing, by comparison, is still in its infancy. There have been pockets of saltwater fly fishers along the East Coast, most notably the Saltwater Fly Rodders of America, founded in 1962 in Elwood "Cap" Colvin's tackle shop in Seaside Park, New Jersey. When I started plying salt water with the long rod in the early 1980s, saltwater fly fishers were still a rare breed except in the Florida Keys. There were no saltwater fly-fishing magazines and very little had been written on the subject.

However, over the last two decades saltwater has become the fly-fishing industry's fastest-growing sector. There are several reasons for the increased interest, but the comeback of striped bass ranks at the top. Successful fisheries management practices and harvest limits brought the striped bass back from the brink. Their remarkable recovery has provided coastal fly-rodders the opportunity to catch a magnificent game fish for most of the year.

As fly fishers become more successful, we look for greater challenges, as in any sport. Perhaps it's to catch more fish or bigger fish, more selective fish or greater fighting fish. Greater fighting fish is what got me hooked on tuna. At first I targeted the smaller inshore tuna, bonito and false albacore. You would be hard pressed to find a fish more selective than an Atlantic bonito or, pound for pound, a stronger fighting fish than a false albacore.

My trips to Florida in search of trophy false albacore often rewarded me with shots at their slightly larger cousin, the blackfin tuna. More recently I graduated to targeting bluefin and yellowfin tuna, an extreme sport if ever there was one. It is hard to describe an all-out tuna blitz, with acres of water being pushed by predators spraying bait up to 5 feet in the air, water white with foam, creating a whooshing sound like an airplane taking off.

Bluewater fly fishing is our sport's last great frontier. It's exciting and demanding and can be extremely rewarding or extremely frustrating, depending on the outcome. While there are many great bluewater game fish to tackle, tuna are my target species, because for me they are the fastest, toughest, most challenging fish to land on a fly rod.

Fly fishing for tuna is a relatively new sport, with many questions still needing answers and many volumes still to be written. While the opinions and theories of the scientists and captains I interviewed varied greatly, they provided a foundation for me to write this book and I am greatly indebted to them.

Targeting tuna has taken my sport to a new level and added much to my enjoyment of fishing, but it hasn't totally replaced other types of fly fishing. I still love the rise of selective brown trout to a dry fly that I have tied. I'm still in awe of bluefish for their tenacity. I still enjoy a midwinter retreat to stalk the ghosts of the flats in the skinny warm waters off some Caribbean island. But nothing gets my adrenaline pumping like chasing tuna.

Just finding tuna in our vast oceans is a major accomplishment, and many of the captains I've had the pleasure to fish with have both pioneered and perfected this art. Once the tuna are located, getting them into fly range and getting them to take a fly requires the skill of the captain and the angler. In my opinion, once you hook a tuna your whole view of fly fishing changes. Until you have done it you can't fathom their speed, power, stamina, and heart. I hope you give tuna a try. I guarantee that you'll never forget your first.

I hope that this book generates interest in fly fishing in general, answers a few questions, causes a few smiles, and raises awareness of the plight of tuna stocks worldwide, especially bluefin tuna. And I hope that it helps in some small way to raise interest in protecting these magnificent creatures for future generations to enjoy, both as sport fish and table fare.

Appendix: Guides and Fly Tiers

Guides (from north to south to west)

Massachusetts

Captain Jaime Boyle
P.O. Box 1986
Edgartown, MA 02539
(Martha's Vineyard)
508-922-1749
Jaime@boylermaker.com

Captain W. Brice Contessa
P.O. Box 3665
Edgartown, MA 02539
(Martha's Vineyard)
508-962-7959
wbricecontessa@hotmail.com
www.contessaflyfishing.com

First Light Anglers
Captains Nat Moody,
Derek Spengler
31 Main Street
Rowley, MA 01969
978-948-7004
tuna@firstlightanglers.com
www.first-light-anglers.com

Northeast Anglers
Captain Joe LeClair
13 Cranberry Way
Marion, MA 02738
508-748-2656; 774-263-2675
flyfishsalt@hotmail.com
www.flyfishsalt.com

On Line Charters
Captain Chris Aubut
1266 Drift Road
Westport, MA 02790
305-797-5442
flyfishwpt@aol.com
www.flyfishwpt.com

Captain John Pirie
7 Kingsman Lane
Hamilton, MA 01936
978-468-1314
www.olfc.com

Captain Tommy Rapone
Edgartown, MA 02539
(Martha's Vineyard)
508-922-1754
tjrapone@yahoo.com
http://fishingthevineyard.com

Ripe Tide Charters
Captain Terry Nugent
5 Great Pine Drive
Bourne, MA 02532
riptide@riptidecharters.com
www.ripetidecharters.com

Shoreline Guide Service
Captain Bob Paccia
56 Beech Street
Bridgewater, MA 02324
508-697-6253
captbob@shore-line.com
www.shore-line.com

Slam Dance Charters
Captain Steve Moore
59 Grant Street
Concord, MA 01742
978-287-4039
slamdancecharter@hotmail.com
www.slamdancecharters.com

Captain Jeff Walther
42 Harwich Road
Orleans, MA 02653
508-240-6602
captainjeff@stripedtease.com

Rhode Island

Early Bird Charters
Captain Dave Preble
64 Courtland Drive
Narragansett, RI 02882
401-789-7596
fishearlybird@cox.net
www.earlybirdcharters.com

Prowler Charters
Captain Al Anderson
7 Jean Street
Narragansett, RI 02882
401-783-8487
ahatuna@aol.com
www.prowlerchartersri.com

The Saltwater Edge Fly Fishing
Company
Captain Corey Pietraszek
561 Thames Street
Newport, RI 02840
401-842-0062; 508-509-3978

Connecticut

Captain Steve Bellefleur
65 Farmholme Road
Stonington, CT 06378
860-535-4856

Lauren "B" Charters
Captain Steve Burnet
1114 Flanders Road
Mystic, CT 06355
860-572-9896

Captain Ralph (Sandy) Noyes
19 Turnpike Park
Norwich, CT 06355
860-886-9212

New York

Finchaser Charters
Captains Frank Crescitelli,
Anthony Grassi
260 Aspinwall Street
Staten Island, NY 10307
717-317-1481

Captain Chris Hessert
251 West 89th Street
New York, NY 10024
917-531-4783
chrishessert@yahoo.com
www.manhattanfly.com

Captain John McMurray
609 Laurelton Boulevard
Long Beach, NY 11561
718-791-2094

Captain Joe "Maz" Mustari
732-888-9669
MazMan@TalkAmerica.net

New Jersey

Outback Charters
Captain Bill Hoblitzell
252 Pond Road
Freehold, NJ 07728
732-780-8624
Biloutback@aol.com
www.outbackfishingcharters.com

Captain Al Ristori
1552 Osprey Court
Manasquan Park, NJ 08736
732-223-5729
cristori@aol.com

Shore Catch Charters
Captain Gene Quigley
732-831-1768; 732-600-3297
Flyfishcharters@aol.com
www.shorecatch.com

North Carolina

Fintastic
Captain Dick Harris
167 Happy Indian Lane
Kitty Hawk, NC 27949
252-261-8394

Sea Creature Sportfishing
Captain Steve Coulter
P.O. Box 189
Hatteras, NC 27943
252-995-4832
seacreature@mindspring
www.seacreature.net

Bermuda

Gringo Charters
Captain Joey Dawson
9 Old House Lane
Spanish Point, Bermuda HM01
441-295-3500

Playmate Charters
Captains Keith Winter,
Kevin Winter
4 Mill Point Lane
Pembroke, Bermuda HM05
441-292-7131 (Keith);
441-799-8862 (Kevin)
playmate@logic.bm

Florida

Captain Scott Hamilton
18334 Jupiter Landings Drive
Jupiter, FL 33458
561-745-2402
www.flyfishingextremes.com

Captain Ken Harris
P.O. Box 2914
Key West, FL 33045
305-294-8843
fishfinesse@aol.com
www.fishfinesse.com

Captain Rush Maltz
46 Bluewater Drive
Key West, FL 33040
305-304-5671
captrush@odysseafishing.com
www.odysseafishing.com

On the Fly Charters
Captain Jeff Burns
21067 Fourth Avenue East
Summerland Key, FL 33042
305-745-4199
kwonthefly.@aol.com

Alabama

Captain Mike Thierry
P.O. Box 502
Dauphin Island, Alabama 36528
251-861-5302
CapThierry@aol.com

Louisiana

Custom Charters, LLC
Captain Tommy Pellegrin
102 Parnell Drive
Houma, LA 70360
985-851-3304
highlifefishing@cs.com
www.customchartersllc.com

Paradise Outfitters
Captains Scott Avanzino,
Lance Walker
P.O. Box 611
Venice, LA 70091
985-845-8006
Avanzino@yahoo.com
www.paradise-outfitters.com

Reel Peace Charters
Captain Peace Marvel
P.O. Box 392
Venice, LA 70091
985-534-2278
www.reelpeace.com

Texas

Gulf Coast Offshore Adventures
Captain Charlie Stetzel
1802 Matthews Street
Houston, Texas 77019
713-805-4262
cstetzel@flash.net

Custom Saltwater Fly Tiers

Blue Ridge Fly Fishers
Blane Chocklett
5524 Williamson Road
Suite 20
Roanoke, VA 24012
540-563-1617
www.blueridgeflyfishers.com

Rich G. Murphy
25 Warren Street
Georgetown, MA 01833
rgmfxbt@aol.com

Teddy Patlen
198 Westminster Place
Lodi, NJ 07644
973-772-1312
Tedpat090@yahoo.com

David Skok
27 Coral Avenue
Winthrop, MA 02152-1133
617-846-0698
dave@dswskok.com

Index